FOCUS *FORWARD* LEADERSHIP

Maximizing Profits in the Artificial Intelligence Age

JOHN ROBERTSON

INDIE BOOKS
INTERNATIONAL

No part of this publication may be reproduced or distributed in any form or by any means without the prior permission of the publisher. Requests for permission should be directed to permissions@indiebooksintl.com, or mailed to Permissions, Indie Books International, 2424 Vista Way, Suite 316, Oceanside, CA 92054.

The views and opinions in this book are those of the author at the time of writing this book, and do not reflect the opinions of Indie Books International or its editors.

Neither the publisher nor the author is engaged in rendering legal, tax or other professional services through this book. The information is for business education purposes only. If expert assistance is required, the services of appropriate professionals should be sought. The publisher and the author shall have neither liability nor responsibility to any person or entity with respect to any loss or damage caused directly or indirectly by the information in this publication.

ISBN-10: 1-947480-51-0
ISBN-13: 978-1-947480-51-3
Library of Congress Control Number: 2019934191

Leadership ID™, Align3™, and Focus-Forward Leadership™ are pending trademarks of John Robertson

Designed by Joni McPherson, mcphersongraphics.com

INDIE BOOKS INTERNATIONAL, LLC
2424 VISTA WAY, SUITE 316
OCEANSIDE, CA 92054

www.indiebooksintl.com

To my wife, who allowed me to be a focus-forward leader,
and to our sons and their wives,
who are our focus-forward leaders for the future

ALL THE BEST !!!
TO ONE OF THE
BEST ??

Oct '2

CONTENTS

FOREWORD

Businesses are fascinating. They thrive in every kind of situation imaginable. It does not matter whether they are large or small. From large airplane assembly lines and small manufacturing facilities to retail outlets and service organizations, it is always enchanting to observe the way business leaders solve their daily problems.

To see an aircraft come together on the assembly line is captivating. So is the experience of seeing a machine build special connectors or watching a stack of cloth twelve inches thick transform itself into uniforms without being touched by the human hand. It takes a myriad of these things to keep America going. It also takes a countless number of companies to make those things happen.

America is successful because of its ingenuity, but the thing that differentiates a highly efficient and profitable company from an outstanding one is leaders with a purpose.

I have observed leadership from the large-business point of view, the small-business point of view, and the government point of view. All organizations have common issues. They must complete plans and programs on time. They have competing priorities for resources. They have financial strains that force decisions away from where they want to go. They have competition that requires constant attention and face many other situations too numerous to mention.

The need I hear about most often is not about the challenges of operating a business; it is about the lack of leaders available to help run the business. I don't believe it is actually about the lack of leaders. In my experience, leaders are in great abundance. What business leaders are really asking for is leaders who can lead leaders. They want leaders who can lead to a purpose not an end result such as production goals or increased profits.

The challenge of finding leaders who can lead leaders, i.e., focus-forward leaders, is as real today as it ever was. Today it is even more consequential. The evolution and impact of artificial intelligence on companies and their leadership at every level will be magnified in the coming years. Maximizing profits will require leaders who can lead leaders, who see a purpose in the future better than they can see the future themselves. It will not be easy. It will be hard to make the changes required.

Executive management studies, now more commonly called leadership studies, were brought to the fore by Peter Drucker. He was the recognized authority and expert on management by objectives in corporations. Over the years, the subject of management by objectives has evolved into the subject of leadership.

Today leadership, as a topic, supports many different situations and fulfills many different purposes. We read about the responsibilities of leadership, we read about theories of employee engagement, and we read about what it takes to be a good leader: all of the same subjects that Pete Drucker started talking about many years ago.

Very little is written about how to lead leaders. Leaders who lead leaders provide a greater purpose to accomplish. There is no greater need to be fulfilled, especially as a CEO. This book is a work to open that discussion.

CEO is a broad term. For this book, the term CEO includes leaders at every level, beginning with small mom-and-pop stores on Main Street. It includes the leaders of middle-market organizations that must continue to be relevant in the marketplace and large corporations with operations around the world. Whatever the situation, this book is for the top leaders at every level of business who are challenged to increase the performance of their organizations.

Leadership as a term is amorphous. It appears in a variety of ways and is uniquely situated in every company. At the lower levels of a company, it is about the success of a particular effort. At the upper levels of a company, it is about the success of the company. At the lower levels, actions (in terms of what someone must do as a behavior or a metric or technique) are effective and functional. At the top, no one answer covers all situations.

Leadership at the top is an approach to complex, multifaceted situations that requires both the skills of leadership and the art of a master craftsman. It is like carving a perfect statue in the midst of a tornado full of rattlesnakes. Indeed, leadership at the top has so many facets that the leader must find a trail through the fog in the confusion of a whirlwind. As a result, CEOs have a completely different set of metrics that define success.

Most leadership studies, books, and services are focused on making better leaders. It is not the intention of this book to rewrite the many leadership lessons that have been shared over the decades. I salute the variety of well-known resources that have made it their work to develop great leaders. All of us in America are better for their efforts and the efforts of those who have followed.

Instead, this book attempts to build on the often-unrecognized factor of who is leading whom. It is the task of top leaders to direct the forces within the company to meet the challenges of an ever-evolving marketplace. It is the challenge of leading leaders.

Focus-forward leadership, or the art of being a CEO, is a top priority for every company. In my own experiences and in the many situations I have observed, most top-level leaders are chosen for what they have done and not for what they will do. They are chosen in the hopes that they will do something good for the company.

I have been in such a situation. My promotion from lieutenant colonel to colonel in the U.S. Air Force was amazing. In a short twenty-four-hour period,

I changed from a person who was accomplished at doing one thing well to being recognized as the person who had *all the answers* and who knew exactly what to do and where to go under a multitude of competing priorities.

How did this miraculous anointing of wisdom and insight occur? It didn't. I was merely promoted based on what I had done. It took me a while to understand what I needed to do.

This is in no way meant to disparage the U.S. Air Force. It is what all organizations do. I have observed it in mom-and-pop stores, start-ups, with entrepreneurs desiring to move to the next level, and even in higher-level organizations pursuing growth.

Leaders demonstrate that they can lead as they successfully complete a project or series of projects. They demonstrate that they can focus inside the company to reach a desired outcome. They work on a single goal with a set of people performing tasks around a single project with a limited set of data and a single outcome in mind. They must interact across functional lines, but their real task and focus is the success of their efforts for the company.

When leaders are promoted to CEO, everything changes. Suddenly, old priorities are offset by new information. What once was a single task is now multiple tasks. What was once a single priority is now a set of multiple priorities, each one as important as the other. What once required a single outcome now requires multiple outcomes. What once relied on a single data point now has multiple data sets to balance and prioritize. And what once was an inward focus is now an inward and outward focus that must also consider the multiple requirements of competition, customer experience, and market presence.

This outlook is what I was thrust into as a colonel and the outlook I still encounter today as I lead my own businesses. It is what every CEO is thrust into, no matter what size or type of company. Leaders know how to lead themselves and they demonstrate they can lead a project to completion, but it is a very different task when it comes to leading leaders and accomplishing tasks through other leaders. It does not matter whether it is a large or a small organization. Every organization struggles in its efforts to find leaders who can lead leaders.

It is with this perspective that I encourage you to read this book. When a person is promoted to the top position of an organization, he or she should already be well accomplished in the talent and competencies of the field, and should already have proven capable of getting things done through other people. The next transition to prepare for is how to stop being a highly skilled and successful project manager and how to start being a CEO.

In the new position as CEO, leaders must demonstrate that they can be successful at leading leaders. There is no training for that conversion. There is no peer group that comprehends how to be a CEO; every experience and situation is different.

This book is the beginning of a set of three designed to help CEOs and others in top leadership positions. Hopefully, you will gain the insight to adjust and understand the challenges that are before you.

It is from this great desire for your success that I wrote this book. Let your wise decisions help you and your company avoid the trap of having to learn in the unmerciful cauldron of misjudgments and mistakes that affect the company's future.

I wish you all the best.

> John Robertson, Col., USAF (Ret.)
> CEO, Focus-Forward Leadership
> Leadership ID and Align3

PART I

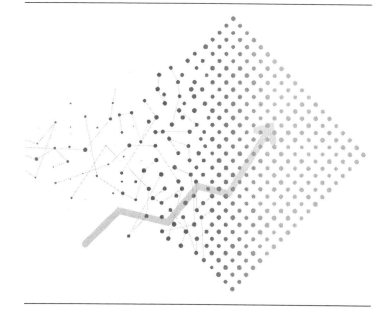

Why Focus-Forward
Leadership Matters

CHAPTER 1

They Didn't See It Coming

I t was Boxing Day, December 26, 2004, and a beautiful morning at Patong Beach on Phuket Island, Thailand. The sun was shining, the temperature was about 80°F, and the waterfront was filled with tourists lounging beneath colorful umbrellas. All in all, a perfect day in the midst of a perfect winter vacation at this seaside resort.

Then, unexplainably, the water in the bay retreated. Everyone stopped to gaze at this strange event. Then it struck. A wall of water more than fifteen feet high moving at 500 miles per hour crashed into the beach and drove inland for a half mile. More water continued to rush in. Tons of fast-moving seawater in a series of huge waves crushed everything in its path. Survivors later reported the seawater was relentless.

In the blink of an eye, this blissful scene of serenity and peace was now a fight for survival. Debris of all kinds swirled and rearranged everything from deck chairs to local economies. Water overturned cars and destroyed hotels. Families were separated, businesses were disrupted, and chaos reigned. What happened? A tsunami. It was later named the Boxing Day Tsunami. *No one saw it coming.*

Tsunamis Are Powerful

Tsunamis are powerful, and they are known for their invisible start. Except for the seismology reading that tells of a major change deep under the sea, there is no visible evidence of the destruction coming. NOAA, the American National Oceanic and Atmospheric Administration, monitors the ocean for sudden displacements in the sea floor. It could be a tectonic plate shift, a landslide, or volcanic activity.

The Pacific Warning Center in Hawaii knew that an earthquake had taken place but there was confusion about its size and magnitude. There was no tsunami warning system in the Indian Ocean. The people on Patong Beach did not know it was coming.

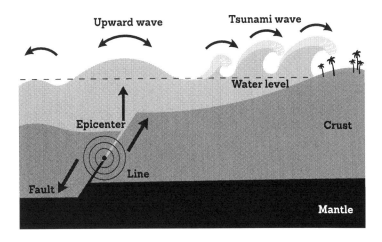

As shown in the graphic, a tsunami wave increases in height as the shock of the disturbance rebounds off the sea floor. As the tsunami wave nears the shore, the shock waves rebound more quickly, causing the ocean's waves to grow higher and higher. By the time a tsunami wave reaches land, the wave is very high, moving very quickly, and transporting enormous amounts of water.

At Patong Beach, the impact was massive and very destructive.

Business Tsunamis

Today, we hear similar tsunami warnings in the business community, but there is no one central voice like NOAA. Instead, there are many voices, often providing conflicting information. But when a tsunami hits, it rocks the business world with many of the same effects as the Boxing Day Tsunami at Patong Beach.

The most recent business tsunamis were the housing bust and financial crises of 2008 and the dot-com bust of the year 2000. Like literal tsunamis, both had beginnings in circumstances that went practically unnoticed.

The 2008 financial crisis started very quietly. Some say it was the result of mistrust between banks. Other say it started with the Graham-Rudman act in 1986 when banks were allowed to invest in complicated investment vehicles called derivatives. Facts point to the derivatives.

Banks used derivatives to provide subprime loans for home mortgages. After 1986 and for the next twenty years, derivatives became hot commodities and were traded like stocks by many, including hedge funds and brokerage houses, such as Lehman Brothers and Merrill Lynch. Their investors included insurance companies and pension funds, among others.

Then, on September 15, 2008, the tsunami struck; Lehman Brothers declared bankruptcy and Merrill Lynch had to be rescued by the Bank of America. The housing crisis followed, with devastating effects. Too many loan defaults overwhelmed the banking system. Many people lost their homes. Investment banks went out of business, hedge funds collapsed, and the real estate market in some places devalued as much as 38.5 percent.

Prior to the bust, many in the financial media proclaimed the benefits of new housing starts and new homeowners. There were also many doomsayers who derided the irresponsibility of the financial markets. Conflicting information creates confusion and raises questions: who to believe?

The innocent never saw it coming. The informed could not stop it.

Every Tsunami Starts With A Silent Earthquake

Another silent earthquake had a very inauspicious beginning in the 1960s. It was simply a design to help large contractors work more quickly with the agencies in the Department of Defense. It did not look or feel like an earthquake when it started. It was just a quiet ripple that was eventually named the internet.

When the public was introduced to the internet, it was like learning about a car. We did not even know how to get it started. Then we fell in love with it, and soon it became essential to our lives. As it gained acceptance, the tech community began providing the public with such things as email for free. Investors began to see opportunities for building immense wealth. By 1997, it seemed every dot-com effort was successful on a large scale and could be projected to be profitable because of the massive number of potential customers.

After the Taxpayer Relief Act of 1997 was passed into law, dot-com investors went wild with company stock offerings (IPOs or Initial Public Offerings). IPOs often drew in big money. As is typical, successful business ideas are frequently copied, and it seemed every new dot-com IPO offering had the same business plan, which was to take command of a business sector through the rapid capture of the business network and sell direct, without the added costs of a middleman.

Business tsunamis begin quietly and have devastating effects, even when the business plan is developed by very smart businesspeople. The bloom quickly came off the rose of the dot-coms in early 2000. The dot-com bust was devastating. As many as 45 percent of dot-coms disappeared. Of those that survived, most lost 90 percent or more of their value. Amazon, a rock star today, saw its stock decline from $100 per share in April 1999 to $6 per share in September 2001. Today it has rebounded, but many others have not.

Most could not see the tsunami coming, and they don't see the new ones forming.

New Tsunamis Are Forming

Business tsunamis hit industry and business sectors independently as technology is developed. Even with warnings sounded by academics and other experts in their fields, CEOs tend to think they are prepared. In the end, every business tsunami must be handled independently and uniquely by every individual business in America and around the world.

An artificial intelligence tsunami is quietly forming with each new technology idea that serves to make our lives better and our activities and pursuits more convenient. Like the unsuspecting beachgoers at Phuket, many leaders are unaware of this hidden obstacle to their success. Just as the housing bust of 2008 had a quiet start with Graham-Rudman and the dot-com bust had a quiet and unassuming start as an unintended consequence of a tax relief bill, this next tsunami has not yet been recognized, either.

Let's look at the often unnoticed and ubiquitous business of personal transportation. Just like the other tsunamis, this earthquake occurred with little notice.

There was no warning; businesses did not see it coming.

It began when the Apple iPhone was introduced in January of 2007. In the beginning, the iPhone simply seemed to be the new toy on the block. It was a more fun, convenient phone. It did not start out as the smartphone we know today. It had no support for third-party apps, no GPS, no SD card support and no real "smarts" as we think of them when we think of smartphones today. But it quickly gained enthusiastic followers who liked its ease of use and convenience. Apple welcomed the enthusiasm and expanded the phone's capabilities in sub-sequent generations (well, except adding SD card support, which remains an Android-only feature to this day) to meet their consumers' requirements.

◆

An artificial intelligence tsunami is quietly forming with each new technology idea that serves to make our lives better and our activities and pursuits more convenient.

◆

A little less than two years later, in December 2008, Travis Kalanick was sitting in an internet technology conference. He, too, was excited about the iPhone. During the conference, he had an idea about how to lower the cost of providing limousine car services using his iPhone. It was simple: "Call a car service with your iPhone." His idea changed the world of limousine service providers and then the world of the taxicab companies. What Travis began with an idea he called UberCab in March 2009 launched as Uber in San Francisco in June of 2010.

Uber's entry into the personal transportation or ride-hailing space had the same effect as a tsunami. The world of the cab driver turned upside-down. Everything in the streets was suddenly different. Riders were walking around cabs and getting into shiny new cars that did not look like cabs. Suddenly the cab companies were sitting in traditional taxi lines, but they were not moving. All the cars *around* them were moving and taking their rides with them.

They did not see it coming.

What for years had been a scene of serenity and peace and stability for the cab companies was now chaos and a fight for survival. And oh, what a fight it has been. The fight for survival has gone from city to city and town to town, and from regulation to regulation. In the end, cab companies settled into a new niche; it is not as attractive as the one they previously occupied.

Uber, meanwhile, is now a household name in sixty-three countries around the world. Now we travel and talk about getting an Uber. We even schedule that Uber in another city, travel there, walk out of the airport, and get into the car, all coordinated with the aid of our smartphones. In fact, if you are an Uber rider, Uber can track you and provide a car for you anytime you want one. But it all began with Travis Kalanick in December 2008 with an iPhone and a little-noticed idea, which created a silent earthquake, which became a tsunami.

Tsunamis have no warning. Companies will not see them coming.

Technology In Waves

A tsunami's destruction is not just caused by the first big wave, although that is very destructive. The real devastation occurs in wave after wave of water and debris that fills every inch of the subsequently flooded landscape.

The coming artificial intelligence tsunami will visit wave after wave of technological change upon us, much like the waves in an ocean: in this case, an ocean of data. These waves are the precursor ripple waves of a huge tsunami called artificial intelligence. This tsunami will change every facet of our lives in the next few years.

The artificial intelligence tsunami will hit with such force and effect that it will engulf business in countless ways. Like the personal transportation business, this tsunami will overwhelm every industry it hits. People will adjust, and consumer requirements will be met, but businesses that are not prepared will be swept away. New businesses with an advanced technology model that meets the needs of the consumer will step into the breach.

Like the impact of the iPhone, the artificial intelligence tsunami is currently a series of quiet offshore earthquakes. Everyone is looking, but no one sees. These earthquakes are born out of technology innovations that have occurred over the last twenty-plus years. These innovations have come in little-noticed waves that added convenience to our lives and advanced our society.

Today, everyone can easily see the impact of these technology waves. We talk online through a host of different mediums, such as Facebook, Snapchat, Twitter, email, and other messaging apps. We buy online from a variety of stores such as Amazon, Wayfair, eBay, and many others. We manage our money online through our banks and send money to others through PayPal, Square Cash, Venmo, and Google Pay. Technology has made our lives faster, easier, and perhaps more convenient.

These technology waves prove that the artificial intelligence tsunami is near. The way companies will be challenged with new ideas and new technology applications is difficult to imagine. What seems so common today is in for more big changes tomorrow. New solutions are introduced daily. There will be more ways to talk, more ways to visit, more ways to shop, more ways to travel, more ways to think, and perhaps even be more kinds of money.

Focus-forward leaders must *see it coming* for their business sector. We know that the tsunami wave will be bigger than any of us can imagine. The Boxing Day Tsunami was bigger than anybody could have imagined. It swept away the unprepared, but companies and structures that were built to withstand the forces of a tsunami recovered to do business again.

Focus-forward leaders must do the same. They must prepare for the worst, the most disruptive events, the most unexpected, so they can recover to do business again. However, even with all of their preparations, when it *does* hit their industry, they will say:

"It was bigger and more powerful than we expected."

CHAPTER 2

How Big Is It?

Just so you know, I am from Texas. In Texas, we brag about *big*. Distance, for example, is defined as miles and miles of nothing but miles and miles. In fact, when we are driving in Texas, it isn't about miles; it's about hours. We never worry about the miles. After all, everyone knows that it is farther from Houston to El Paso, Texas than it is from El Paso to San Diego.

If you are in Houston, it takes about ten-and-a-half hours to drive to El Paso. It takes about the same amount of time to drive to San Diego, except you have to go through three states to get there. From Houston, it is only three hours to Austin and four hours to Dallas or San Antonio.

So in Texas, we are used to big. But that does not even come close to talking about how big the artificial intelligence tsunami is going to be.

Perhaps it is helpful to think about it this way. Imagine yourself sitting on the edge of space. If you could ever find that spot, you would still be looking at a vast void that makes up the universe. Some scientists say the universe is continually expanding. It is so big, so vast, even *they* cannot grasp the size and depth of it.

The same is true for artificial intelligence. We cannot grasp the size and depth of it. But we can find ways to talk about it. The field is broadly defined by three phases: artificial narrow intelligence (ANI), artificial general intelligence (AGI), and artificial superintelligence (ASI).

The development, study, and application of artificial narrow intelligence began early in the 1950s. It has now grown into a competent stage, with its capability limited to one functional area, such as data analysis. By 2025, this stage will have grown into the artificial *general* intelligence stage, with the capability to reason, solve problems, and provide abstract thinking at the human adult level. By 2050, it is estimated that artificial superintelligence will have the ability to surpass human intelligence across all fields.

Today, the business community is watching and wondering as artificial intelligence develops. It is like beachgoers watching the ocean retreat at Patong Beach. Everyone is gazing in amazement, wondering what is about to happen.

In the words of the financial giant UBS: "Artificial Intelligence will become a massive sector that unleashes a torrent of financial opportunities and will provide industry captains, both government and corporate, with unparalleled technological power."[1]

It is bigger than we think and will be more than we expect.

---

1 "The Evolution of Artificial Intelligence." www.ubs.com/wm. January 2017. https://www.ubs.com/hk/en/wealth-management/thinking-ahead-in-asia/2017/new-dawn.html.

More Than We Expect

Perhaps it will be like the morning of May 18, 1980.

Everything was peaceful that morning. The mountain had been doing its usual rumbling as it had for the last eight weeks. Everyone—the University of Washington, the U.S. Geological Survey, the mountain residents and those interested in the possibility of a volcano blowing its top—was watching. They thought they were safely protected. Even the lone vulcanologist assigned to the ridge camp sending daily reports was six miles away. The 7:00 a.m. report that morning was consistent with past reports.

♦

By 2050, it is estimated that artificial superintelligence will have the ability to surpass human intelligence across all fields.

♦

Then it happened. At 8:32 a.m., the top of Mount St. Helens in Washington State blew away. *It was much more than they expected.*

What had been a beautiful mountain with a conical top at 9,600 feet just seconds before was now a gaping horseshoe-shaped crater that would later be measured (when it was safe) at 8,300 feet. Within fifteen seconds, 1,300 feet of mountain, rocks, and trees, including the north face of Mount St. Helens, disappeared. The eruption blew superheated gas and rocks out of the mountain at near supersonic speeds. Everything within eight miles of the blast, including the ridge camp monitoring station, disappeared.

A second vertical explosion followed quickly after the first. It sent a cloud of ash and gasses twelve miles into the air. Within twenty minutes, hot mud from the melted ice and snow was moving at ninety miles per hour through the rivers west and southwest of the mountain. The shockwave leveled almost everything for nineteen miles beyond the blast zone.

The Mount St. Helens eruption touched almost the entire southwest side of Washington state and much of the western side of Oregon. Ash rained down for more than nine hours. It blocked the sun and turned on streetlights in Spokane 300 miles away. Sewage systems were clogged, air traffic control was shut down, fifteen miles of railway were damaged, 185 miles of roads needed replacement or repair, and more than 200 homes were destroyed. Fifty-seven people died. In the end, more than 540 million tons of ash covered seven states and approximately 2,200 square miles. Damage to buildings, timber, and agriculture was estimated at $1.1 billion.

It was more than they expected.

Like the Mount St. Helens blast, the artificial intelligence blast will be more than expected. Its impact will change everything. The rumbling has started. Many are watching. Many think they are far enough away to be safe. Many say times are different.

And they are.

Times Are Different

When it comes to the artificial intelligence tsunami, today we have smarter and faster software and computers; better, larger, and more flexible worldwide data storage capabilities; and a huge profit potential driving investor participation. The forward momentum is breathtaking.

Enterprise Management 360˚ is a leading company that serves information technology professionals. In a June 13, 2018 article, the organization says that by 2025 it expects artificial intelligence to move from rules-based systems through solutions-based on knowledge and experience, to computers that have the capacity to reason, negotiate, and interact with humans and other machines.[2] All this in just seven years. It will be the same as the top blowing off a mountain.

It will move so fast that we will not be able to escape it and *it will be bigger than we expect.*

There Is No Time to Waste

The question for every focus-forward leader is, will they be prepared like Texas in the year 1900 or Texas in 2017?

Let's take a trip back in time to the year 1900. Sailors first detected a tropical storm well east of the Windward Islands on August 27. It entered the Caribbean Sea on

---

[2] Talwar, Rohit, Steve Wells, Alexandra Whittington, April Koury, and Helen Calle. "The 7 Stages of the Future Evolution of Artificial Intelligence." Enterprise Management 360˚. October 05, 2018. Accessed December 05, 2018. https://www.em360tech.com/tech-news/tech-features/artificial-intelligence/

August 30 and passed over the Dominican Republic as a weak tropical storm on September 2. It hit Cuba on September 3 and stayed there for three days. On September 6, the storm entered the Gulf of Mexico and strengthened into a Category 4 hurricane with 145 mile-per-hour winds. Early on September 9, 1900, two weeks after it was first observed, the hurricane made landfall on Galveston Island near present-day Jamaica Beach, Texas.

They knew it was out there. They didn't think it would be as bad as it was. When it hit, they could not escape. The storm surge was eight to twelve feet high and inundated the entire island. Every house was damaged. More than 30,000 people were left homeless on an island of 38,000. At least 3,600 homes were destroyed; the rest were rendered uninhabitable. An estimated 6,000 to 12,000 people died.

It was bigger than expected.

Hurricane Harvey

More than 100 years later, on August 25, 2017, Hurricane Harvey hit the Texas coast with fury. It was the first Category 4 hurricane to make landfall along the Texas coast since Hurricane Carla in 1961. Hurricane Harvey caused $125 billion in damage, primarily from more than forty to sixty inches of rain as the system slowly came ashore and stalled as a rainstorm. The storm surge was also as high as twelve feet. Hundreds of thousands of homes were flooded, and again, more than 30,000 people were left homeless. But more than 17,000 people were rescued from the floodwaters, and there were only 106 confirmed deaths.

The impact of Harvey was severe, but this hurricane did not result in the loss of life that occurred with the Galveston flood of 1900. With the help of the NOAA satellite, emergency planners knew how big the hurricane was and when and where and how long it would remain. People watched it form and grow in the Gulf of Mexico. They boarded up their homes and headed inland to wait out the storm. Emergency response crews were prepared, and thousands of others joined in the effort to rescue people from the floodwaters. A year later, in 2018, cities and towns and people all along the Texas Gulf Coast are still recovering from the storm.

Even with all the preparation and technology advances over the past 100 years:

It was bigger than expected.

Businesses must combine the Texas experiences of 1900 and 2017 and the Mount St. Helens experience of 1980 to plan for the artificial intelligence tsunami. Businesses know they can withstand a direct impact for a short time, but what happens when the top blows off, or it rains for days and days? Businesses know how to get ready for past storms, but every storm is different. It is impossible to imagine how big the artificial intelligence storm will be.

It will be bigger than expected.

The first technology waves are already upon us.

The First Technology Waves

Tsunami waves grow higher and higher as they approach the shore just as the artificial intelligence waves are growing higher and higher as they approach. Here are four scenarios to consider.

- **One.** What is the largest car rental company in the world that owns no cars? Answer: Uber. The organization has a presence in sixty-three countries. Uber can be at your house or business, usually within five minutes. You can expect a clean car and a friendly, courteous driver who will take you wherever you want to go, even if it is in your local neighborhood. Taxi and car rental companies all over the world have not yet found a way to effectively compete.

- **Two.** What is the largest vacation home rental company in the world? You got it: Airbnb. This company facilitates more vacation and business rentals than anyone else, yet they have no budget for maintenance or cleaning. You and I can see and inspect each location from the comfort of our home. The owner usually provides a well-equipped unit with a wide selection of amenities, and Airbnb is assured that it will be ready for the next guest. Hotels the world over are already competing for this travel dollar.

- **Three.** What home security company started from scratch just a few years ago and yet has no staff? Answer: The Ring doorbell company. It has sold millions of units to home buyers who install them personally and monitor the cameras through their smartphones. It would be reasonable to think that Ring will soon add staff and a revenue stream by monitoring the doorbell feeds for homeowners. Home security companies of all types are learning how to compete in this new technology world.

- **Four.** How does an ordinary dairy farm become extraordinary? Answer: Through disruptive digital technology. Cameras and other technology sensors now monitor everything from feed production to milk production. In some cases, they even use facial recognition technology to determine if a cow is getting sick. Sound simple? Try making it work with 1,000 head and two milkings per day.

Here are other scenarios to consider.

- Farming is now reliant on technology advances. John Deere has been prototyping the use of driverless tractors for twenty-plus years.

- Weather satellites are turning forecasting into an expectation, not a prediction.

- Apple is now using a robot called Daisy to disassemble 200 iPhones each hour.

- Companies are exploring cashier-less stores.

- Surveillance technology is becoming common. By 2020, in China, facial recognition will be used by the state to influence (control) behavior through their Surveillance Star, which will be linked to a social credit system.

The first waves of the Artificial Intelligence Tsunami are already upon us.

It is already bigger than we expected.

And new applications are just around the corner.

An Application For Every Challenge

Every future challenge, real or perceived, will be provided through a digital response with advanced data techniques leading the way. Artificial intelligence will bring great abundance, but it will also require businesses and individuals to develop new models with digital solutions.

To use an old Texas phrase, "This thing is giving us more than we can say Grace over, and it isn't even started good yet." Every industry and every job will be affected. Research tells us not to worry; only an estimated 5 percent of jobs will be eliminated.

But almost 100 percent of jobs will be affected. Another statistic says we will lose 1.8 million jobs and gain 2.3 million jobs over the next

◆

The coming tsunami requires each proactive, focus-forward leader to see how artificial intelligence will affect his or her industry.

◆

five years. The problem is these millions of people will need to be retrained.

It is bigger than we think.

The coming tsunami requires each proactive, focus-forward leader to see how artificial intelligence will affect his or her industry. These leaders must understand the size of the challenge of the artificial intelligence tsunami in order to maximize profits in the days to come.

CHAPTER 3

Focus-Forward Leaders

L eadership remains critical to success and profits. That is the conclusion that reached out from the pages of The Conference Board's April 2018 survey report, "C-Suite Challenge: Re-inventing the Organization for the Digital Age."[3]

The Conference Board, Inc. is a nonprofit business research group with approximately 1,200 members worldwide. Founded in 1916, it is well known for providing reports on the leading economic indexes, the U.S. Consumer Confidence Index, and the CEO Confidence Survey. Their research and analysis reports have been so accurate that they are widely quoted and respected by investors and policy-makers worldwide.

Confirming that focus-forward leadership is a must to maximize profits, The Conference Board summed up the top three CEO conclusions in their April report. Leaders need to: (1) be found and kept, (2) rise to the challenge of artificial intelligence, and (3) develop the next set of leaders—true challenges in every respect.

---

[3] "C-Suite Challenge™ 2018: Re-inventing the Organization for the Digital Age." The Conference Board. April 2018. https://www.conference-board.org/c-suite-challenge2018/.

Items one and three are age-old challenges that make leaders want to say, "Move on; nothing to see here." But when we add artificial intelligence to the mix, the challenge is renewed in a very different way.

Artificial intelligence requires that focus-forward leaders must be found and kept in order to maximize profits.

Focus-Forward Leaders

In 2010, three former NASA engineers were intrigued by the development of smartphones that had more processing power and better sensors than our most expensive satellites. Their passion was to develop an inexpensive means to continuously monitor earth from outer space.

In 2013, these idealistic guys, in a Silicon Valley garage, completed and deployed a trio of three tiny satellites named Alexander, Graham, and Bell. The development cost was a whopping $7,000. Chris Boshuizen, Will Marshall, and later, Robbie Schingler saw an opportunity to reach into outer space via the smartphone technology of the day. Their crazy idea turned out to be very successful.

They began by building very small satellites that used cheap smartphone components and sensors that were readily available on the open market. Being engineers, they called what they were doing agile aerospace and put all the components into a housing the size of a shoebox. Their satellites became better and less expensive with each new cell phone revision because of mass-produced smartphone parts and sensors.

Their success attracted venture capitalists. Today, their idea is a business. The company, now named Planet Labs, launched twenty-eight small satellites in 2014. Each satellite, still about the size of a shoebox, went into low orbit from the International Space Station. By the end of 2017, 130 low-orbiting satellite shoeboxes were producing and transmitting enough data to produce high-resolution images of every place on Earth, *every day*.

Today, their shoebox constellation of satellites observes more than 100 million square miles of the world, produces 130,000 images, and processes 5,200 gigabytes of data daily.

Planet Labs can now provide data for a wide variety of applications. Their data is readily available and relatively inexpensive. It is boundless, limited only by the imagination of those who need it. Here are some examples.

- They can monitor shopping mall traffic or provide data about weather patterns.

- They can provide data to assist in natural disaster events such as hurricanes and volcanic eruptions.

- They can provide data about worldwide agricultural crop yields and data to assess drought conditions anywhere in the world.

- They can continuously monitor onsite safety for construction operations.

- They can follow container shipments across the sea, in ports of call, or traveling on the world's highways.

In the past, such data had to come from one of the giant companies, which acquired it through a more labor-intensive process. Planet Labs was their artificial intelligence tsunami.

Planet Labs changed everything, from how data is collected to the price for its release to the speed of the reports to reactions in the marketplace. Planet Labs has given everyone the ability to see the world as it changes. Its leaders feel the company has an obligation to nongovernmental organizations, corporations, scientists, and journalists to observe and understand how the world is changing every day.

All of this was done by three focus-forward leaders who saw a technology solution that became an earthquake. Businesses around the world need to embrace and encourage these kinds of focus-forward leaders. Otherwise, these leaders will become their next competitors and may start the next industry earthquake.

Focus-forward leaders must be found and kept.

Companies and organizations must have focus-forward leaders who can lead with an eye on the future today and develop focus-forward leaders who can make that future a reality tomorrow.

Focus-Forward Leaders Must Develop Focus-Forward Leaders

It began in 1973. OPEC, the Organization of Petroleum Exporting Countries, raised oil prices by 200 percent. This action created a crisis and a shortage of gasoline in the United States. At that time, two-thirds of America's oil imports came from OPEC.

One focus-forward leader refused to accept anything less than a solution that would give oil independence to America. This proactive, focus-forward leader centered his thoughts on new and better ways of offsetting America's requirements for OPEC oil. His ideas included and influenced solutions such as increased use of hydraulic fracturing ("fracking") technologies, horizontal drilling, and development of shale resources. Through his influence and development of two generations of focus-forward leaders, many successful initiatives were started and proved fruitful.

However, in 2008, six presidents later, America was still too dependent on OPEC oil. Oil still amounted to two-thirds of America's trade deficit. More importantly, there was no coordinated energy plan to take advantage of the new developments in technology. His initial goal remained the same: oil independence for America.

This focus-forward leader put forth a new initiative: a plan for energy independence. The goal was to use new technologies that were not available in 1973 to create a greater offset to oil dependence through the influence of industry and government leaders. The plan included engaging leaders at the local, state, and federal levels to increase awareness about alternative fuel sources, such as natural gas, wind, and solar. It also put forth the idea of creating a tremendous number of jobs and the opportunity to put America first in energy exports of both oil and liquified natural gas.

In 2008, the plan set a goal of cutting America's OPEC dependence in half in ten years with the impact of new technologies and new ideas, such as engaging the independent trucking fleet more advantageously. Achieving such a goal would cut imports by 2.5 million barrels per day. By 2013, just five years later, United States oil imports were down by 50 percent, and the nation was listed as one of the fastest-declining importers of oil in the world. In 2018, the United States became a net exporter of oil products.

Natural gas resources increased because of the development of shale technology. Liquid natural gas is now being exported to other countries, especially in Europe. Electric power is provided by solar and wind farms that stretch from Texas to Canada and from the East Coast and the West Coast.

This focus-forward leader's efforts, through other focus-forward leaders that he has developed, trained and influenced, have resulted in a solution that is working and will work well into the future.

Today T. Boone Pickens, at ninety years young, is still looking for focus-forward leaders and solutions. He works according to the belief that leadership is the quality that transforms good intentions into positive action, and it turns a group of individuals into a team. It took forty-five years and perhaps two generations of focus-forward leaders to develop an OPEC solution. We will not have that kind of time in the artificial intelligence age.

◆

Focus-forward leaders must develop focus-forward leaders to rise to this challenge.

◆

Focus-forward leaders must develop focus-forward leaders to rise to this challenge.

Rise To The Challenge of Artificial Intelligence

Consumer demands and the dynamic worldwide marketplace feed persistent competition that never sleeps. Software modeling, algorithms, and machine learning only serve to speed up the demand for more real-time information from enthusiastic companies that can use data to further their business models.

Space, media, retail, manufacturing, and almost every other business sector are being reimagined. Focus-forward leaders are using the tools they have at hand along with their ingenuity to forge new ways of meeting their customers' desires.

IBM, once was known for making the best typewriters in the world, stopped making typewriters in the 1980s. Their focus-forward leaders changed to computers, then to delivering services, and now they are changing again. They are leading the artificial intelligence revolution with Watson, their entry into the artificial intelligence age. They are not alone: Apple, Microsoft, Amazon, and Google are all challenging the status quo by contributing their thoughts and ideas to tomorrow's solutions.

T. Boone Pickens, IBM, and a trio of engineers on the West coast used focus-forward leaders and focus-forward thinking to keep their companies well directed and positioned for the future. Fortunately, the new generations of focus-forward leaders are comfortable with constant change and have the desire to innovate. The Artificial Intelligence Age will be an age of innovation, driven by new technologies.

Innovation

The challenge of innovation in the artificial intelligence age is pervasive. It cuts in many directions all at once. Innovation can bring abundance and profits and/or expense and failure. More importantly, innovation is not just a CEO or top management task—it is an *everyone* task. Leaders must be open to someone else in the company having a better idea.

In another section of the April 2018 The Conference Board report, it was noted that CEOs need to create a culture of innovation in order to prosper and survive. A culture of innovation means everyone is recognized for the success of a plan or a goal. It means everyone in the company is connected to the future and invested in the results that are required to make it happen. It means engaging in cross-functional ideas to encourage cooperation and promote risk-taking.

CHAPTER 3

Innovation is a must as a company moves into the artificial intelligence age. Changes will occur too fast to rely on just one position or one team to provide new ideas. Leaders must learn to develop trust and communicate better to engage every level of the organization to contribute what they see and know. Both leaders and employees must each accept the responsibility to be transparent and effectively engage with one another. It will take focus-forward leaders who develop focus-forward leaders and organizations to meet this challenge.

The powerful business incentives from the world-wide reach of innovation and artificial intelligence will propel markets and industries into The Artificial Intelligence Age. These incentives for profit cannot be ignored. Focus-forward leaders must be visionaries who see the needs of tomorrow with innovative solutions today. Just as importantly, they must supply a solution today as they innovate a solution for tomorrow. It requires focus-forward thinking.

◆

The powerful business incentives from the worldwide reach of innovation and artificial intelligence will propel markets and industries into The Artificial Intelligence Age.

◆

Focus-Forward Thinking

Focus-forward thinking is about imagining how to use the technological advances of today to help companies provide products and services that will be of great benefit to mankind. It is about the ability to see what we cannot yet see—helping that person in a wheelchair to walk, or helping those who cannot hear today to hear tomorrow.

Focus-forward thinking means that even though others cannot say a word, we can help them talk. It means that even though others are blind, we can help them see. And it means that even though *we* cannot drive in a rainstorm, we can still *drive* in a rainstorm. Focus-forward thinking means the ability to see a greater potential to fulfill the purpose for our company and the lives we touch.

Most leaders cast an occasional glance toward their purpose, but the demands of their businesses and their leadership habits keep them looking at today rather than their purpose going forward. It is very difficult to see the future when you are sitting in the saddle looking at the south end of a northbound horse. The speed of competition and the demands of technology no longer allow businesspeople to ride this way. They must look to their future purpose, focused forward with their leaders and with their thinking.

The challenges of the artificial intelligence age require focus-forward thinking to help leaders to: (1) define and reshape their company from within to meet the outer reality that will be known as the artificial intelligence age, (2) develop focus-forward leaders at the top and throughout the company to be ready for the innovations of the future, and (3) diligently apply the five focus-forward leadership action items that we will discuss in the following chapters.

Focus-forward leadership is about the artificial intelligence age. As focus-forward leaders, we must position ourselves and our companies to withstand successfully the rigors and challenges of the coming tsunami. It will come when we least expect it. It will be bigger than we expect. And it will require focus-forward leaders to develop for tomorrow what is not here today.

To *maximize profits* through focus-forward leadership, leaders must master the application of the action items examined in depth in the next part of this book.

PART II

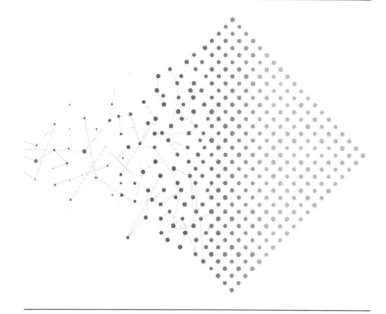

What Focus-Forward Leaders Must Master

CHAPTER 4

Lead To What You Believe

ACTION STEP ONE: Lead With A Picture In Mind

The year was November 2000. The company had just acquired Honeywell. Retirement was upon him, but the board wanted him to stay on a little while longer to complete the integration. The iconic leader of General Electric, Jack Welch, responded by staying on to complete the picture he had started twenty years before. When he led, it was about the destination. When he retired in September 2001, he left an enduring legacy.

It all began in 1960 when Welch joined GE as a young PhD chemical engineer fresh out of college. When he was promoted to CEO in 1981, the company dealt in manufacturing; when he left, it was one of the nation's top financial services companies. When he began, GE had a market capitalization of $3 billion; when he left, it was $424 billion. When he began, it was a successful company; when he left, it was among the most highly valued companies in the world. How did he do it?

Welch's definition of leadership begins and ends with taking people where he is going. When he entered the CEO's office in 1981, he knew where he was going and what he wanted to do. All he had to do was tell his people what his dream was, where the company was going and how they could participate. It is a time-honored way of doing business. It resulted in very high value and long-term profits.

Creating A Picture With Words

Mark Miller and Lucas Conley reinforce this point in their new book *Legacy in the Making: Building a Long-Term Brand to Stand Out in a Short-Term World*.[4] They tell us that in today's short-term world, the traditional rules for building and maintaining long-term brands are losing their power, and we should return to them. Jack Welch's legacy suggests they are on the right track. But this is easier said than done.

Describing where the company is going and how employees can participate is perhaps one of the most difficult challenges CEOs and top executives face. In fact, it is something they struggle with constantly. The struggle centers around who/what the company is now and who/what does the company need to be five years from now. It is a question of personnel, assets, capabilities, and an accurate focus on the future.

Unfortunately, that is the opposite of what most company CEOs are challenged to do today. Investors want results quickly. They are not always in it for the

---

[4] Miller, Mark, Lucas Conley, and Yvon Chouinard. *Legacy in the Making: Building a Long-Term Brand to Stand out in a Short-Term World*. New York: McGraw-Hill, 2018.

long haul. By contrast, the age of the master's degree and quarterly reports were not Jack Welch's measures of success, even though they were all the rage in terms of leadership and success formulas during his tenure at GE.

Warren Buffett of Berkshire Hathaway and Jamie Dimon of JPMorgan Chase are beginning to share Jack's point of view. In a joint op-ed on June 6, 2018, in *The Wall Street Journal* titled "Short-Termism is Harming the Economy," they note an "unhealthy focus on short-term profits at the expense of long-term strategy, growth, and sustainability."[5] Buffett and Dimon go on to say that businesses should wean themselves from short-term results like quarterly estimates. Instead (and let me paraphrase) *they should do the things that make America great and leave an enduring legacy everyone can be proud of.*

I am not sure what happened at GE after that day in September 2001 when Welch retired. But since that fateful retirement day, GE's stock price is down 80 percent (as of the time of this writing). GE has been delisted from the Dow Jones Industrial Average, a position the company had held since the average began in 1896, and today struggles for its place in the corporate world.

Perhaps its CEO, John Flannery, who took over in August 2017, will heed the legacy of Welch. After a year on the job, Flannery is already reorienting GE to

---

[5] Dimon, Jamie, and Warren E. Buffett. "Short-Termism Is Harming the Economy." *The Wall Street Journal.* June 07, 2018. Accessed November 09, 2018. https://www.wsj.com/articles/short-termism-is-harming-the-economy-1528336801.

a new future. His biggest task is to lift GE to a new level and provide a destination that everyone wants to work toward.

Communicate A Destination

Welch taught us that CEOs must communicate their dream effectively. They must communicate what they want the company to accomplish. Then they must believe in it so passionately that the rest of the workforce adopts it as their calling as well.

Just a few years ago, the idea to do this was called a vision. Today we find vision statements posted on almost every company's website, break room walls, and in other conspicuous places where they can be displayed. In the beginning, vision statements communicated. Today, they look good for the stockholders and investors. We need another way to communicate the destination.

Modern visions are often communicated via word pictures or purpose statements. Whatever we call them, they must build a picture with words to tell employees what the company wants to accomplish in the world in which they work. Such pictures communicate a reason to work and a destination everyone can buy into. Clear word pictures share where the company is going and what the future looks like.

Let's go back to the early days of Apple. Steve Jobs started Apple with this destination word picture: "To make a contribution to the world by making tools for the mind that advance humankind." That is a good word picture because it says what he wanted to accomplish in the world in which he and the company work. It compels buy-in. It specifies the action to be taken, a future that can be seen, and results to be realized. Employees who were a part of Apple at that time certainly did buy into the vision.

◆

CEOs must communicate their dream effectively. They must communicate what they want the company to accomplish. Then they must believe in it so passionately that the rest of the workforce adopts it as their calling as well.

◆

Here is Apple's vision statement today:

> *Apple designs Macs, the best personal computers in the world, along with OS X, iLife, iWork and professional software. Apple leads the digital music revolution with its iPods and iTunes online store. Apple has reinvented the mobile phone with its revolutionary iPhone and App store, and is defining the future of mobile media and computing devices with iPad.*

That is a good statement for the stockholders, but limited in its application. It is *not* a destination word picture that employees need. What is it in Apple's vision statement that an employee should accomplish, other than to be an employee?

Similarly, Bill Gates of Microsoft began with a good destination word picture. Again, let me paraphrase: *a computer on a desk and in every home and every office.* It was clear and concise. Every employee

43

could take action toward the vision. They could see themselves in the future and realize results for themselves.

Today Microsoft's word picture has changed, but the company's leaders did not make the same mistake as Apple. Their destination word picture still compels buy-in. It says: "We believe in what people make possible. Our mission is to empower every person and every organization on the planet to achieve more."

Bravo! Microsoft gets it. They are still giving their employees something to accomplish. In a nutshell, Jobs and Gates and their start-up companies were *destinations everyone could buy into*.

These forward-focused leaders communicated a picture of what was possible with everybody working together, and as a result, both built very successful, high-value organizations. They recognized the old saying: "A picture is worth a thousand words." In business, we might also say it is worth millions of dollars.

Lead with a picture in mind.

A Picture Is Worth Millions Of Dollars

In March 2009, a University of Pennsylvania psychology study revealed that visual learners convert words to pictures in their minds. Stated another way, when such learners say or hear a word, their minds convert them into pictures. For example, if I say *apple*, a visual learner will see the fruit in their minds. They don't see the letters that spell apple. The apple one person sees may be a different size or shape or color than the one another person sees, but their minds see an apple nonetheless.

Studies claim that most of the population learns visually. Gates and Jobs proved that time spent developing a phrase to describe the future with word pictures is time well spent. It is the CEO's responsibility to turn the future into a word picture the rest of the company can identify with. Some CEOs are able to do this more easily than others.

One CEO who does this easily is Donald Trump. (This is not about politics; it is about a CEO operating in a very public setting. He offers a very good view of how a billionaire CEO thinks and operates.) Trump began, even before he was President (CEO) of the United States, by providing a compelling destination word picture. He said let's "make America great again." As with the apple, although we may have different ideas about how one looks, we all know what an apple is. The same is true with this statement. In our minds, we each have a clear idea of what a *great America* looks like. It is a clear destination picture, and the country voted for that picture.

♦

Trump began, even before he was President (CEO) of the United States, by providing a compelling destination word picture. He said let's "make America great again."

♦

When the CEO is successful in creating a destination word picture that everyone can adopt, it becomes an enduring legacy that everyone will strive for. In the case of Welch at GE, it was, "We bring good things to life." For Jobs, it was about "advancing humankind." For Gates, it started as *computers everywhere.*

Each of these CEOs leads with a picture in mind.

An Important Step

A destination word picture is an important step to maximizing profits in the artificial intelligence age. It is imperative that CEOs develop a clear and concise word picture for employees to buy into. This is more than an exercise to fill a square on the corporate HR checklist; the word picture communicates a future outcome.

It also sets the boundaries for companies to work within as they move forward. Companies without a clear destination in mind often take side roads hoping for a better result.

It is not unique that a company would try its luck in another endeavor; they do it all the time hoping to produce better profits for the company. Stories abound about companies acquiring other companies to expand their reach into new markets. Often these stories end with less than stellar results.

The artificial intelligence age will require a clear idea of the future, stated in the form of a destination word picture that sets boundaries. Creating this picture must involve the employees to make the company successful.

Lead with a picture in mind. This act is an integral part of the art of being a CEO.

The Art Of Being A CEO

The art of being a CEO is about *leading with a picture*—about the ability of the leaders to transfer their ideas to others who buy into the picture and contribute their experiences to the picture to make it even better. In effect, they become an extension of the CEO and help others in the organization to invest their time, energy, and talent as well.

♦

Lead with a picture in mind. This act is an integral part of the art of being a CEO.

♦

The art of being a CEO is centered on defining and remaining focused on a destination word picture. It is a simple concept. With this in mind, the CEO sets boundaries, encourages employee engagement, and forms a set of ideas that become targets—extraordinary results to achieve. In turn, extraordinary results drive the significant day-to-day actions and everything else needed to exceed expectations and maximize profits. With this framework, the destination word picture becomes the CEO's enduring legacy gift to the company.

Deviations from the destination word picture are what keep CEOs awake at night.

It Keeps Them Awake At Night

What *keeps them awake at night* is how to create a predictable organization that can solve today's challenges while providing a path to the destination word picture. Every CEO knows that today's decisions affect the employees' actions and tomorrow's outcomes.

In my life experience, the CEO and top executives in many companies often feel like riders on the top deck of a double-decker bus. They can see where they want to go, and they fully intend to go in that direction, but they do not have access to the accelerator, brakes, or the steering wheel.

The bus driver controls the accelerator, brakes, and the steering wheel. The bus driver is dealing with what is in and on the road right now. The bus driver cannot see over the hill or around a curve. The bus driver cannot see the destination. In fact, in many companies, the bus driver does not know the destination, only turning quickly to the left and to the right as each situation arises.

For those on the top deck, every turn can be a maddening detour from where they expect to go. Only when both the top deck and the bus drivers have the same destination in mind and coordinate the stops and turns will the trip become much less chaotic.

The task of every CEO and top executive team is to build a destination word picture that both the top deck and the bus drivers know, understand, and believe in.

As the CEO, action item number one is absolutely true. We must:

Lead with a picture in mind as we lead through others.

CHAPTER 5

Lead Through Others

ACTION STEP TWO: Hire Focus-Forward Leaders

Several years ago, a sales company that had many locations throughout the United States was struggling with year-over-year poor sales performance results. The sales offices had many of the typical excuses: turnover, variable sales cycles, and not enough office support were among them. The CEO was having none of it and challenged the general manager to fix the problem.

The general manager had been appointed to this recently established position after having been with the company for many years. While the CEO was responsible for the overall management of the company, the general manager position had been established to handle the responsibilities of daily operations and to report to the CEO.

The CEO and the general manager both liked and had great respect for each other. Complicating the situation was the fact that they were remotely located from one another and also had very different leadership styles.

As in many companies, revenue increase was the CEO's defining metric for success. For the CEO, success was to be gained through a team of highly capable individuals who generated the highest revenues. This put the focus on top individual performers. The individuals who generated the highest sales revenue were thought to produce the best profits, no matter where they were in the company.

For the general manager, revenue was not the primary success measure; profit was. The general manager looked at success through the lens of overall company profitability. This was the metric for job success and the metric the CEO was using to judge job performance. In the general manager's view, each office must produce the highest profit to its best capability.

In one particular location, the CEO was most aware of an employee who happened to be the highest-volume producer in the whole company. The location manager (whose metric was profits and who reported to the general manager) and the high-producing employee (who had the CEO's ear) were in constant conflict because the sales producer had an unusually high level of expenses relative to sales volume. The salesperson's activity *did* generate higher revenues but also produced lower-than-expected profits for the office.

The general manager had hired the location manager because this person had a history of developing very efficient, productive, and profitable offices. In this situation, the location manager was unable to produce the results they wanted. The CEO's focus on sales performance with the top producer left them little room to change the culture or actions of the team. It also created bad habits on the part of other sales team members and resulted in lower office productivity and profitability. The situation needed to be resolved.

In private discussions, both the CEO and the general manager agreed that the desired goal was high profits. As focus-forward leaders, they recognized their common ground was high profitability from profitable offices with high revenue. By focusing on profitability as a common outcome, the general manager and the CEO refined their understanding of success. High profits rather than high revenue became the new standard.

The CEO *hired a focus-forward leader to maximize profits.* Today, they work to propel the company into a more profitable future.

Hire Focus-Forward Leaders To Propel A Company Forward

No amount of planning or organization or any of the other tricks of the leadership trade can focus to move a company forward. Only a leader can propel a company forward. Focus-forward leadership requires the leader of the company to know the destination word picture and to have the right leaders in the C-suite and below to deliver the message to the rest of the workforce.

Otherwise, as we say in Texas, you'd better keep your saddle oiled and your horse ready, because you're the only one running the show.

Some CEOs and top executives hire the first leader available. Typically, these new leaders are chosen because they are problem solvers and decision makers who are highly talented and competent in their field. They get things done on time and within budget. Because of their daily discussions, CEOs and top executives assume that each has a clear understanding and that they are working toward the same destination. This is a common assumption, but not an accurate one.

Leaders from other companies may be relying on lessons learned from past experiences and events with other companies rather than a clear picture of the destination of their current company. They may always have a great answer, but it may be "borrowed" from another company's best practices rather than their own clear picture of where the CEO wants to go.

Iconic CEOs and top executives are remembered because they provide a clear picture of a single destination and they hire the right leaders to get there. They drive the company to success through focus-forward leaders who look into the future, stay on task, and chart a profitable course.

Iconic Leaders Hire Focus-Forward Leaders

Leadership is the most talked-about and the most confounding function of every business. Perhaps it is because leadership is different for everyone. Some leaders fit one company and do not fit another. Some leaders fit a company for a season but do not fit for a lifetime. Others fit better in a centralized, structured environment rather than in the dispersed decision-making and cross-functional teamwork philosophy that is more common today.

♦

... as we say in Texas, you'd better keep your saddle oiled and your horse ready, because you're the only one running the show.

♦

In his book, *Good to Great*, Jim Collins emphasizes that it is first "who."[6] Who are the leaders needed at every level of the company?

At the top must be the focus-forward leaders who will help the CEO define the destination word picture for the future. Near the front lines must be leaders who can "carry the water" and explain how employee actions are an important part of the destination word picture. The focus-forward leaders in the middle interpret and demonstrate that picture for everyone to see.

In an ideal world, we would start with the right leaders and then build a company. However, most companies do not start out that way. They start with an idea and use the people they have to grow. They rarely stop to find the right leaders along the way to help them become more successful. And then, after they are successful, these organizations tend to keep the same leaders around, even after they have outgrown them.

---

[6] Collins, James C. *Good to Great: Why Some Companies Make the Leap...and Others Don't*. New York, NY: Collins, 2009.

I have yet to find many leaders who are ready to *bet their company* on a change to their current leadership team.

We must hire focus-forward leaders that fit the position for the future. Unfortunately, most leaders hire people they like rather than leaders who can propel things forward. Here is an axiom to remember: *Who we are says how we lead; who we hire says how they lead.*

This action step (*Hire Focus-Forward Leaders*) cannot be ignored. CEOs must have the right leaders in place to survive the artificial intelligence tsunami that will roll over companies in the next few years. Let me illustrate what can happen without the right leadership team in place.

An Example Of The Need To Hire Focus-Forward Leaders

A regional company with about twenty locations was born during the dot-com boom of the 1990s. It was a very popular go-to solution for electronic products. The organization became very profitable because they were friendly and provided excellent expert advice. As the excitement over computer products waned, however, so did this company's ability to maintain sales. Leadership's first solution was to open more stores in better locations. It was a good effort, but sales did not meet expectations. Then they remodeled all their stores; that did not meet expectations, either.

After several years of frustration, an analysis of their customer preferences revealed that their customer base had changed. Yesterday's customers wanted friendly expert advice; today's customers were smart and educated, so they wanted value and functional capability. They liked friendly expertise, but expertise had to give way to closing the sale.

One solution from the analysis was to change hiring expectations. The company was hiring salespeople who were friendly experts and did not like confrontation (which includes asking for the sale). For the company, asking for the sale was vitally important, because its products were now a commodity that could be purchased anywhere. Salespeople had to do more than just provide value and functional capability; they had to ask for the sale.

◆

CEOs must have the right leaders in place to survive the artificial intelligence tsunami that will roll over companies in the next few years.

◆

The CEO got it. He agreed with the analysis. He himself was a person who always asked for the sale. The vice president of sales, a good friend of the CEO who by this time had been with the organization fifteen years, did not get it. He was a friendly expert who did not like confrontation. He hired people he was comfortable leading: people like himself.

The CEO knew a change was required. The dilemma: how to change the sales format and selling techniques without losing his company. He proceeded carefully and inserted himself into the sales hiring process. After a year, about 50 percent of the sales force had changed from friendly experts to friendly salespeople who asked for the sale. The CEO saw sales increase by approximately $1,000,000 per store. He was very pleased and assumed that the new hiring techniques would continue. He returned to relying on the VP of sales to continue the process.

The CEO did not change the VP of sales. (*Who we hire says how they lead.*) Nor was there a C-suite to provide focus-forward leadership.

A year later, the CEO's hiring practices had faded away, and the old hiring practices had resumed. Today, sales are down. The company exists as one of many in a very crowded and competitive market, and the CEO is once again frustrated and worried. It is our hope that the company attracts focus-forward leaders before the coming artificial intelligence tsunami washes over it and leaves such a mess in its wake that the company cannot recover.

Every company must learn how to recognize focus-forward leaders who understand the destination and fit the company culture. In the early stages of a company's life, most CEOs have the uncanny ability to spot focus-forward leaders. They hire based on their gut. In Texas, we have an old saying: "Follow your gut before you follow your head." It works until the company outgrows the CEO's ability to hire everyone. Then CEOs must rely on others to spot leaders for them.

For me, leadership recognition came out of a challenge as a young Air Force captain in the Pentagon many years ago. It was my job to work with high-level leaders (they all were colonels or generals) to sharpen my leadership skills. On one occasion, I asked a two-star general how and why he made the decision to assign a particularly detailed analytical task to a particular person.

His answer was interesting. He said, "I believe he has a lot of potential but not very much confidence in his ability to get the job done." The general said, "I highlighted him with that task to report to me to lift him above his current supervisor. I want to see if my senses are correct. If I am right, we should see an outstanding report in a very short time. Especially since the supervisor is going to be on vacation over the next few weeks."

◆

In the early stages of a company's life, most CEOs have the uncanny ability to spot focus-forward leaders.

◆

As it turned out, the general was very pleased. The report was above expectations, and he used this person for many other special assignments. I asked the general how he knew that person would perform so well. He told me; "You have to learn to size people up. Some people have big holes in their screen doors, and others are bright as a new penny. You just have to figure out which one is which."

I asked him how. He said, "It ain't rocket science," and left me to figure it out for myself.

Finding Focus-Forward Leaders

Finding focus-forward leaders is an important task, but it isn't rocket science. It does not take a fancy college degree to get the right people in place. What it does take is persistence, determination, and a clear idea of what you want to accomplish. It takes a clear picture of where the company is going and a person with the right performance attribute assets to excel at a particular job to help you get there.

When you put your destination into words that someone else can build a picture around, you simply have to ask if someone buys in. Once people buy in, then ask them how they are going to get there. If you like their answers, you will like their results. They are focus-forward leaders.

Companies must hire focus-forward leaders to create focus-forward organizations. But CEOs can't stop there. They must also guide their leadership team to interpret the destination word picture, both in terms of what they will do now and what they will strive for in future years. This requires each member of the leadership team to determine and declare what their role is and what they will do to get there. Every focus-forward leader must do his or her part to lead the company to its destination.

CHAPTER 6

Lead to A Destination

ACTION STEP THREE: The Profit You Maximize

Yogi Berra, the legendary Yankee catcher, was known for his memorable quips. His quirky sayings transcended baseball. Some included, "It ain't over 'til it's over," "Baseball is 90 percent mental; the other half is physical," and, "If people don't want to come to the ballpark, how are you going to stop them?"

Berra had a humorous and effective way of communicating. He once talked about a St. Louis restaurant this way: "No one goes there anymore. It's too crowded." I especially like the one about the sun in left field of the old Yankee Stadium during late-season games. He said, "It gets late early out there." No matter how he said it, people always got the picture.

As leaders, we must do the same thing as Yogi. We must communicate a picture of the future effectively, even when it gets late early out there. Otherwise, let me paraphrase Berra this way: *If you don't know where you are going, how are you going to know if you got there?*

There is a universal law that says we will move toward what we see in our minds. It is true for baseball teams, individuals, and companies. Leaders will consciously and unconsciously make decisions that propel us in the direction of the pictures in our minds. We must be sure that the picture communicates the profit we want to maximize.

The Profit You Maximize

For a baseball team, a picture of winning the pennant should be the profit they want to maximize. For individuals, pictures of what they each want to accomplish in life should be the profit they want to maximize. For a company, a picture of what they will accomplish should be the profit they want to maximize.

Leaders in every situation must communicate the picture effectively to lead to the destination. Decisions made with different pictures create different out-comes, and a fuzzy or unclear picture leaves room for confusion. Only singular, distinct, and clear pictures can maximize profits.

A word of caution: Maximizing profits cannot be a destination. This directive drives the company in two directions at once. One direction is short-term, the other is long-term, and both require different sets of decisions.

When maximizing profits is the destination, short-term profit is often the default result because CEOs need to maximize profits to increase perceived company value. It is their report card. But remember this thesis:

"The profit you maximize is the place you go." Short-term profits lead to a short-term focus, short-term outcomes, and perhaps a short-term company.

Working in businesses that are short-term focused can be frustrating and chaotic. Every day is a new twist and turn in the road. Every day creates reactions to events. What was important

◆

Short-term profits lead to a short-term focus, short-term outcomes, and perhaps a short-term company.

◆

yesterday may not be as important today. Short-term requirements such as cash flow, payroll, needs for product development, unforeseen manufacturing requirements and unintended sales consequences are but a few of the things that can force leaders to react defensively in the short term.

Employees do not like coming to work in a short-term environment. For them, it is like waking up out where the busses don't run. It starts and ends in frustration and confusion.

Leaders who run short-term focused businesses are about as welcome in the office as a tornado on a trail drive. They often keep the staff all tangled up, like a bird trying to build a nest out of barbed wire. The office is constantly busy and constantly interrupted. Nobody is happy; profits are not being maximized.

In the end, short-term profit destinations cannot maximize profits in the artificial intelligence age. It takes a longer-term view and a team to maximize profits.

The Profit You Maximize Requires A Team

The C-suite team, including the CEO, must see the future they are working toward. They must know what their company looks like in that future. Leaders who promote how the company affects the world will build teamwork and generate

◆

Leaders who run short-term focused businesses are about as welcome in the office as a tornado on a trail drive. They often keep the staff all tangled up, like a bird trying to build a nest out of barbed wire.

◆

buy-in from their employees. Microsoft and Apple affected the world with "computers on every desktop" and "advances to humankind." What these teams wanted to accomplish was a picture that affected every employee and the future. They maximized profits along the way. They measured progress with rest stops.

A few years ago, one of my sons and his family were transferred to Kansas City. They had three small children at the time, so my wife and I agreed to keep them for a week while my son and his wife completed the move. At the end of that time, we scheduled a drive to take the kids to Kansas City. It was a long drive, about eleven hours, but we decided that it was better to complete the trip in one day rather than working through the confusion of staying overnight somewhere along the way.

The kids were excited about the destination word picture: their new home in Kansas City and being with their mom and dad again. But that was too far away for them to remain excited for very long. We had to come up with short-term results to keep them engaged along the way. So, we looked forward to rest stops. Pancakes in Waco, stockyards in Fort Worth, the National Cowboy Museum in Oklahoma City, and the airplanes at the Air Force base in Wichita, Kansas were among the interim results we looked forward to on our long drive. These became our benchmarks for progress toward our greater goal. When we finally got to the outskirts of Kansas City, we began to talk about the last rest stop: their new home.

These rest stops proved to the kids that we were making progress. After driving for about seven hours, everyone was ready for some time out of the car. We stopped at a particularly interesting spot near the Kansas-Oklahoma border. When we were ready to get back into the car, one of my granddaughters balked. She had decided we had gone far enough and that we were actually lost. No amount of persuasion could get her back in the car.

In exasperation, I pulled out a travel map and laid it on the ground. Then I gave her a marker and asked her to trace the highway from her home in Texas to Kansas City. We also marked where we were. It helped her see that we were in the right spot. It was an interesting exercise. She actually walked on the map to retrace our journey. After she did that, she was convinced we did indeed know where we were going. We all got back in the car and headed to Kansas City.

The word picture of their new home was the primary motivation for our trip and something worth doing. But without rest stops or results to look forward to along the way, it would have been easy to say, "It is time to stop," or "We are lost," or "We should go in another direction." Instead, we had a clear destination with designated rest stops on a map. We had charted a course and we stuck to it. We accomplished our goal without any unintended side trips.

The same is applicable to organizations. They not only need a word picture of what they want to accomplish but also signposts to mark progress along the way. Leaders must lead people to the destination, and that usually involves rest stops or interim destinations. When we arrived in Waco for pancakes at the Elite Café on the circle, everyone was hungry and excited about our progress.

The same was true for the stockyards in Fort Worth and the museums in Oklahoma City, even though everyone was tired by the time we got to the Oklahoma-Kansas state line. Some were confused, some were tired, and some just wanted it all to be over. But no matter the feelings, the goal to be accomplished was still in sight. We continued to lead to the destination.

The same experiences can be related by companies on their way to a destination that seems too far away. It is critically important to set shorter milestone destinations that everyone can recognize. They are the rest stops along the way. Focus-forward leaders call these rest stops "extraordinary results." They are predetermined points to maximizing profits along the way to the word-picture destination.

If we do not care about maximized profits, we can settle for anything as a rest stop. The only requirement is that it is recognized as an achievement so employees can feel good about what they have done.

The Profit You Maximize Must Achieve Extraordinary Results

Rest stops that we call extraordinary results are specific. They can still be tangible or intangible, but they must be *objective*. They must maximize results (profits). Objective results can have only one interpretation, such as *pancakes in Waco*. Subjective results can have multiple interpretations (such as whether the pancakes in Waco were *good* or *bad*). Both determinations involve pancakes, but only one maximizes profits.

Tangible results are such things as revenue and profitability. Intangible results are such things as being recognized as an industry thought leader or an increasing number of customers referred by outside parties. Both have only one outcome. Extraordinary results take away misdirected actions; they create a more

> ◆
>
> **Objective results can have only one interpretation, such as *pancakes in Waco*. Subjective results can have multiple interpretations (such as whether the pancakes in Waco were *good* or *bad*). Both determinations involve pancakes, but only one maximizes profits.**
>
> ◆

motivated workforce, drive a higher quality product, and maximize profits.

Let's look at Microsoft's journey as an example.

You will recall that Microsoft's picture of the future was a computer in every home and office. Their first extraordinary result or rest stop was a major company that could put their operating system into the company's computer product. IBM was that company. In the 1980s, IBM selected the Microsoft operating system, called DOS (short for Disk Operating System) to run its computers.

Microsoft's next extraordinary result was a broader operating system called Windows. Since the first version, Windows has undergone many improvements and is now in version 10. Other extraordinary results along the way were home and office applications: word processing, spreadsheets, presentations, and publishing tools among them.

Every extraordinary result led toward Microsoft's view of the future with computers on the desks of every office and home. Every extraordinary result leads to maximized profits. Today, Microsoft has fulfilled its original view of the future. Can anyone argue that they are not highly profitable?

The Profit You Maximize In The Artificial Intelligence Age

Now Microsoft is working toward an artificial intelligence future with a destination that calls for empowering every person to achieve more. If its history is any indication, we can look for the company's focus-forward leaders to maximize even more profits as it leads to this new destination with new rest stops along the way.

The profits of the artificial intelligence age will involve both people and computers applying new ideas from both developed and developing technologies. CEOs and top executives must stop and imagine how artificial intelligence will affect their markets and their products. They must start now to develop a clear picture of what their company will accomplish in the artificial intelligence age. New ideas, driven by a vision to accomplish a company's purpose, will provide the ability to maximize profits.

The task of every leader is to understand that the decisions made today affect what will be accomplished tomorrow. And the rest stops leaders define along the way will determine how well they maximize profits in the artificial intelligence age.

In every case, leaders must lead with decisions that multiply.

CHAPTER 7

Lead To Profits

ACTION STEP FOUR: Lead With Decisions That Multiply

I t ended on November 10, 2012. The winningest coach in college football history stepped down. He was not as well-known as the media-darling football coaches in Division I, but this unassuming focus-forward leader had an amazing sixty-year run. He won 489 games, more than any other coach in history. In a small Benedictine school in central Minnesota, John Gagliardi did not have a losing season after 1967.

The question from every CEO in America should be, "How do I create a winning record like that?"

It is often said that Gagliardi taught leadership as much as he taught strategy and tactics. He created high expectations, and he concentrated on winning. But for Gagliardi, winning was not at all costs. His approach was about what he wanted to accomplish. He depended on the players to make good decisions. He taught focus, concentration on critical points, and flawless execution.

For him, winning was when and where to employ the right methods and practices that would win football games.

Gagliardi's practice regimen emphasized execution with flawless repetition. It also included his famous list of noes. Here are several that CEOs might want to consider for their teams.

First, there is *no* single way to do the job. Second, his attitude was, *no* problem or obstacle can stop us. And third, there was *no* other rule than the Golden Rule.

And then he had a list of not-dos. This was another list of noes that were things he and his team would not do. This list could go into the hundreds. Here are a few of them. No recruiting off campus, no excuses, no trash talk, no tackling in practice, and no depending on good luck. Scoring was no big deal (they expected to score). There were also no long practices (ninety minutes max), no blocking sleds or dummies, no athletic scholarships, no compulsory weight-lifting programs, and no whistles. He knew that the path to winning was his to make.

It was always about leading with decisions that multiply.

As a coach, fundamentals and flawless execution were the only things that held Gagliardi's attention. He did not look at fame or opportunities to coach at other schools or how many players went to the National Football League. He wanted every player to be better in every way, every year. His word picture was one of high expectations for every player. He only looked at how to make his players the best for every game. His decisions multiplied his success and created momentum that made him legendary.

Lead With Decisions That Multiply

Decisions that multiply can make your business legendary. Newton's second law of motion deals with the energy from applied force. Newton tells us that when we apply force to something, it moves in a direction. If we apply more force, it will move in the same direction faster. Once an object begins to move, it will continue to move in that direction until and unless something changes its direction. The lesson for us all: Apply consistent force to accomplish a recognized goal to maximize profits.

Here is what is important for a CEO: The force that leaders apply is a decision. Many decisions working in the same direction are a force multiplier. The direction of a decision will be maintained until other decisions change its direction. Stated another way, decisions in the same direction create more force, and that creates more momentum toward maximized profits.

With this valuable insight, the CEO or top executive can multiply the impact of his or her decisions and create momentum to maximize profits simply by remaining consistent.

Just as effectively, but unintentionally, when decisions are out of line with maximized profits, force may be applied in another direction and momentum toward the original goal will decrease. Maximized profits suffer.

All Great Masters Lead With Decisions That Multiply

Ralph Waldo Emerson tells us, "All great masters are chiefly distinguished by the power of adding a second, a third, and perhaps a fourth step in a continuous line. Many a man has taken the first step. With every additional step, you enhance immensely the value of your first."

Emerson's quote is a great, if not subtle, description of decisions creating momentum. It is up to the CEO and top executives to determine the decisions they will make on their path to maximizing profits.

But it is not just the big decisions that create or interrupt momentum. The Law of Decision says that everything we decide is a decision, *even if we decide not to decide.* Every decision confirms a direction and applies force. Force either increases momentum or reduces momentum and resets direction. It goes without saying that reduced momentum does not maximize profits.

Every leader at every level must lead with decisions that multiply. As focus-forward leaders, every action and decision should assure that the decision stays true to the word picture that will maximize profits, even when placed under a spotlight.

Lead With Decisions That Multiply Under A Spotlight

In 1946, Estée Lauder was making creams at home on a restaurant stove and delivering them personally. She was absorbed by the cosmetics business, and every decision she made, whether it was about the product, the salespeople, or the customer, always maximized profits. Lauder was dedicated to making decisions that multiplied.

She pioneered a "free gift to every purchaser" program. It still exists today. She provided free samples at charity functions and other benefit occasions. In the beginning, she even chose her salespeople carefully to "focus on the whole woman" and not just the face.

In 1995, the company issued its first public stock. Its success continues to be outstanding. Today the Estée Lauder company has a clear purpose to accomplish. It is summed up in the phrase, "Bringing the best to everyone we touch." In living their purpose, the leaders of Estée Lauder have made the decision to maximize profits with new products and by acquisition.

In leading with decisions that multiply, the Estée Lauder company puts every acquisition under a spotlight. The acquisition result must answer this question: Are these companies innovating, and have they proven their product is a winner in the marketplace? If you are in the cosmetics industry and want to build a company for acquisition, simply innovate and prove your product is a winner. Estée Lauder will probably want to talk to you.

Lead With Decisions That Multiply To Create Momentum

Estee Lauder is an industry leader enjoying the success of its focus-forward leadership. The organization is maximizing profits because decisions are directed within the focus of the word picture the company is working toward. Leaders have chosen their path to maximize profits. They also have the basis for determining the data they will need to gather and the direction they will travel as they maximize profits in the artificial intelligence age.

Estée Lauder's success and John Gagliardi's success attest to the fact that outstanding focus-forward leaders keep their decisions on only the one path that leads them to what they want to accomplish. A picture of that path might look like this, with each arrow representing a decision.

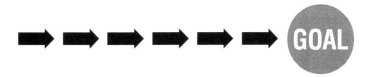

Gagliardi's success was in maximizing good decisions that led to flawless execution that led to maximized wins in the highly competitive environment of a football field. Estée Lauder's success is in making decisions that bring winning innovations to everyone the company touches; that leads to maximizing profits on the highly competitive playing field of the cosmetics industry.

In Contrast, Multiple Decisions Do Not Multiply

Companies without a clear purpose to accomplish make decisions about many things that will (hopefully) improve and perhaps maximize profits. One such company had developed more than thirty franchises of its business idea over the period of about ten years. The initial business model had been quite successful in a very competitive services industry.

The original idea was to consolidate this service sector, control the market, and then sell to the highest bidder. The business plan established their goal in terms of business value, which is a result and not a purpose for working. With this plan in hand, the CEO focused on maximizing profits and allowed any new idea that would increase profits, rather than ideas that would increase their impact on the service sector and expand their control of the market. (As mentioned earlier, maximizing profits is a result, not a purpose.)

In the beginning, the CEO enjoyed good success and franchises sold well. The business value increased. But competition is not to be ignored. Newer, more technologically advanced services began to erode the business plan and change the industry. New franchisees were harder to attract.

To offset losses, the CEO decided to add other products and services based on inspirations to maximize profits for the franchise, but not necessarily for the franchisees. For example, added services required more employees to provide more options for service. But the franchise operators balked at the cost of training and support to roll out the services to their customers.

In frustration, the CEO started developing new lines of business outside of the industry, with other business partners. Employees at the franchise headquarters did their best to maintain the franchise, but without a clear idea of what they were to accomplish, their decisions were often redirected by the CEO.

The CEO's decision path to maximize profits might be represented by the picture below. Each turn of the arrows represents an unfruitful idea or a new line of business. Each turn also represents a new priority and a decrease in momentum rather than an increase in momentum.

Business leaders want momentum toward a predetermined goal. Multiple circles, however, do not follow a direct line to outcomes that support an original idea or a business plan. They do not maximize profits, even if the company enjoys some amount of financial success during side trips.

Every company wants its decision-making process to be a straight line to a goal. This inability to set priorities creates the decision circles described above. Decisions that multiply require setting and sticking to priorities.

Priorities Help Others Lead With Decisions that Multiply

Priorities for decision-making are established by taking into account what a company desires to accomplish (action item one), the leaders it has to direct action within the company (action Item two), and the rest stops along the way (action Item three). Decision-making is aided by a continued focus on spotlight questions that keep every decision centered on outcomes that create momentum. Spotlight questions come from priorities.

In our experience, leaders and their employees generate many ideas on a daily basis. Without priorities, focus on an outcome to be accomplished is easily lost. After thirty days, a high and lofty outcome may give way to the daily urgency and demands of the business. The initial goal may no longer be recognized as purposeful or a path to profits.

♦

Very few companies know how to put together a set of decision-making priorities that will produce a straight line to its goals.

♦

77

The Path to Profits is Yours to Make

The path to profits leads through the forest of daily decisions that may or may not multiply. The path is straight and true if decisions are made with a priority on a clear course of action to accomplish a larger purpose. The path becomes a wandering and meandering trail when decisions provide limited outcomes to achieve short-term successes.

Once again, let me reference a very public CEO, Donald Trump, the President of the United States. His overarching purpose is to "make America great again." This is what he wants to accomplish. His rest stops are centered on the economy and other factors designed to increase jobs and the prosperity of the citizens of this country.

These things can be interpreted in many ways, with many solutions, until decisions are evaluated against his priority statement: "America first." Now, every discussion and every decision his staff and cabinet members make in regard to their actions toward the rest stops are to be centered on this priority.

It is the same for every business: *The path to profits is yours to make.* That path must necessarily lead through the decision forest and answer the questions, "What's to be accomplished? What are our priorities? And what rest stops should be expected along the way?"

◆

It is the same for every business: *The path to profits is yours to make.*

◆

But the guiding action is to lead with decisions that mul-

78

tiply. All of the other facets of a business are irrelevant without focus-forward leaders to make the decisions that propel a company forward with momentum.

The focus-forward leaders' words, decisions, and actions must all line up to provide a picture to the workforce to allow them to see where they are going. The picture creates leadership accountability. Priorities, spotlights, and rest stops reinforce the picture. Words create the outcomes.

CHAPTER 8

Lead to Achieve

ACTION STEP 5: Words Create Outcomes

The day was Friday, June 12, 1987. President Ronald Reagan was in West Berlin to celebrate the 750th anniversary of the city's founding. He was standing before a crowd at the Brandenburg Gate in front of the Berlin Wall. It was an opportunity to continue a process with the Soviet Union that could reduce Cold War tensions and renew negotiations on nuclear arms reductions. More importantly, it was the ideal time and place to champion freedom for the East German people by challenging the Soviets to remove the Berlin Wall.

The Berlin wall was built in 1961 to keep the people of East Germany from escaping to West Berlin and then into West Germany. Since then, it had continued to be a repressive reminder to the German people of the harsh conditions that family and friends endured under the Soviet occupation of East Germany after World War II. During his speech, President Reagan issued a challenge to Mikhail Gorbachev, who was then the General Secretary of the Communist Party of the Soviet Union. Reagan spoke these powerful, famous words, which were heard around the world: "Mr. Gorbachev, tear down this wall."

"Tear down this wall" conveyed a powerful outcome. A little more than two years later, on November 9, 1989, the Berlin Wall came down. Eleven months later, on October 3, 1990, East and West Germany were officially reunited.

Words Create Outcomes

President Reagan stated in no uncertain terms the outcome that his words were to accomplish. He did not ask, and he did not think, "it would be nice if." His words, with passion and certainty, declared an action to be achieved.

Every person leads with his or her words every day, often with passion and certainty. We utter them almost without regard to their impact. Most of us do not take action without thinking and perhaps saying aloud where we are going. We may be going for a cup of coffee or going to lunch or dinner. We may be going home or going to a ball game. Whenever we are going somewhere specific, we speak with clarity and certainty about it.

As leaders, we do the same thing with our organizations. Most of the time, we speak about specific short-term outcomes that produce short-term results. Leaders need to speak about long-

◆

"Tear down this wall" conveyed a powerful outcome. A little more than two years later, on November 9, 1989, the Berlin Wall came down.

◆

term outcomes. That is where the profits are maximized. Short-term words bring quarterly results. Long-term words bring extraordinary results that maximize profits. It depends upon what we want to achieve.

Lead To Achieve

An old adage exhorts us: "What you say is the momentum you create." Long-term words are productive and create momentum toward what the company wants to accomplish. They produce abundance and create very few, if any, decision circles.

Short-term words create quick action. Many leaders like short-term words because these make them feel as if they have a nimble organization that can react to new challenges quickly. In reality, this is a charade. It is the difference between being *productive* and being *busy*. Short-term words create busyness and often stifle momentum because they only answer to the now and not what is to be accomplished over the long term.

Notice the adage does not say, "What you print is the momentum you create." Words and ideas on paper do not create productivity or momentum. Leaders do.

Words from leaders create productivity and momentum. When leaders build word pictures about the direction in which they are going and what they want to accomplish, they are leading to achieve and create productivity toward something.

Words Create Outcomes

The more often leaders talk about the same destination, the more people will buy in and believe they are going on the same journey. When people apply their effort to realizing the words leaders use, momentum is created. More effort applied means more productivity and more momentum toward the desired outcome.

This is exactly what happened after Dr. Martin Luther King Jr. gave his famous "I Have a Dream" speech in Washington, D.C. on August 28, 1963. In his speech, Dr. King called for civil and economic rights and an end to racism in the United States. His words were powerful. They were spoken with passion and certainty. Many bought in and applied their efforts toward pursuing the goal. Today, our society is living the outcome of these famous words, spoken again and again over the past fifty-five years.

The momentum from that speech has seen the rise of African American leaders in every level of American society. Here are three of many examples:

- Dr. Ben Carson became the director of pediatric neurosurgery at Johns Hopkins Hospital and became the seventeenth United States Secretary of Housing and Urban Development.

- Dr. Mae Jemison is an African American engineer, physician, and NASA astronaut; she has flown in space aboard the space shuttle Endeavor.

- Herman Cain is an African American politician, author, business executive, radio host, syndicated columnist, and candidate for the 2012 Republican party presidential nomination. He has served as chairman of the Federal Reserve Bank of Kansas City, on the board of directors of several corporations, and as CEO of the National Restaurant Association.

Powerful words work to accomplish a dream or express an idea that can move nations, societies, and organizations. Leaders must communicate their desired outcome in clear, passionate, determined words that describe the result with a certainty that everyone can buy into.

Words Create Outcomes

Let's go back to September 12, 1962. It was a warm, sunny day at the Rice University campus in Houston. President John F. Kennedy was talking to a crowd of about 40,000 in the football stadium when he declared that the United States would put a man on the moon before the end of the decade. Those very words defined what was eventually dubbed the American "space race" with the Soviet Union.

President Kennedy spoke with passion and certainty about the desire of every American to win the space race by putting a man on the moon. He assigned NASA, the National Aeronautics and Space Administration, founded in 1958, with the task of completing the undertaking before the end of the 1960s.

NASA challenged Wernher von Braun, the leader who developed German rocket technology during World War II and later became the father of space science technology in the United States, to fulfill this task, along with many companies who had to literally invent the technology to put a man on the moon. Together, this team built a seven-year set of rest stops that included everything from propulsion to space food to oxygen regeneration to keep men alive in space.

President Kennedy led to achieve when he spoke the words that set the destination of a man on the moon by the end of the decade. On July 20, 1969, Apollo Eleven landed on the moon.

Words Create Outcomes and A Destination

A destination is part of the reason we all work. Productivity and momentum begin when we have a place to go and a time to get there. Employees engage when they know the destination involves them and they hear it from their leaders.

Leaders must speak about the company's destination. Nothing is more effective than verbal communication delivered regularly with passion, certainty, and determination by the top executives and supervisors throughout the company. These leaders can communicate the destination easily when using the company slogan as encouragement, or as a test to ask about the validity of a new idea. They can communicate it as a priority for decision-making and for actions to encourage efforts around a new task.

We see mission and vision statements posted on the walls and bulletin boards of companies large and small. We see logos on letterheads and other places. Companies do their best to both communicate a brand to the public and to reinforce it to their employees. But leaders cannot depend on a piece of paper to communicate their destination for them.

Written words reinforce the picture, but words on paper do not speak, and destinations do not count until people hear it from their leaders over and over again. When pressing issues are on the table, or if what the company wants to accomplish is the most important parameter to be considered, words determine direction. Words multiply actions that maximize profits. Words grow the company or hold the company still.

Words Create Outcomes

The Great Atlantic & Pacific Tea Company, Inc., was the powerhouse of grocery stores 100 years ago. Founded in 1859, it introduced the first supermarket in 1936 and had nearly 16,000 stores across the United States by the 1940s. After World War II, the grocery business changed, but A&P did not. The original founders could not see a new destination and did not hire focus-forward leaders who could see a new destination. After the founders died in the 1950s, the new CEO vowed to keep A&P a great urban grocery store just as the founders had done.

Upstarts like Kroger, Safeway, and Albertson's all changed the way groceries were delivered through modern and convenient supermarket stores in the suburbs. A&P's leadership stuck with its urban stores. They thought people would still come to town.

Their words did create an outcome, but they did not multiply actions that maximized profits to grow the company. Even when the company went public, they refused to change to the new suburban supermarket concept. By the 1960s, A&P's sales were flat and remained that way.

In July 2015, the company filed for Chapter 11 bankruptcy protection. Today what remains of the Great Atlantic & Pacific Tea Company, Inc. is a little-known chain operating under many different names.

As John Keating tells us in the 1989 film *Dead Poet's Society*, "No matter what anybody tells you, words and ideas change the world." The leaders of A&P needed to hear competition was changing their world. Focus-forward leaders were needed to reorient the company to a new destination. Instead, the A&P leaders used words that drove toward a different, but just as powerful, outcome.

Indeed, the words focus-forward leaders use will change the world, their companies, and the lives of those who work for them. In the future, artificial intelligence will provide a new set of leadership challenges. But it will take leaders in front of workers using words to convey who the company is and what they want to accomplish.

Leaders, Not Computers, Must Use Words to Create Outcomes

Artificial intelligence is currently in the process of learning words, with the goal to understand the written word and derive meaning from it. This project is called *natural language processing*. Microsoft, IBM, and others are focusing on machine learning technology to provide this capability for such things as text recognition, image content, and text translation. As the artificial intelligence age matures, more and more applications of machine learning will affect the words that machines use and how businesses work with one another and with the public.

Words from focus-forward leaders will remain the primary leadership vehicle to set the tone for how well our employees see the future with us. Leaders' words determine priorities and willingness to make decisions. Leaders' words provide a positive means to build trust as we move our businesses into this age of artificial intelligence. If leaders don't use words and computers do, the question will be, who is leading?

Machines still cannot evaluate the future and determine a new destination for business. Machines cannot determine new rest stops or a new priority for decisions. Artificial intelligence may be required to *reinforce* the leaders' words, which set things in motion and propel the company into the future.

In the end, only leaders can propel a company forward. It is up to every focus-forward leader to be sure that the words artificial intelligence uses will fulfill the priorities that drive the decisions that create the momentum that will maximize profits for the company.

Words Create Outcomes

A company's destination must be at the forefront of why employees come to work. It needs to be so commonly understood that every employee can relate it to their work. Some companies *just get it.* These companies have progressed in the art of using words that maximize.

Google, the search engine giant, gets it. In 2016, Google was one of the fifty best companies to work for, according to *Business Insider* magazine.[7] Google says its mission is: "To organize the world's information and make it universally accessible and useful." Google employees are encouraged to find ways to make that happen. Their priority for decisions simply asks, "Does it help?"

In other words, does it help Google to organize the world's information and make it universally accessible and useful? If the answer is yes, then employees, even at the lowest levels of the company, have an opportunity to work on something they can relate to and become passionate about.

Google's focus-forward leadership generates such momentum and enthusiasm, it is no wonder the organization is one of the fifty best companies to work for.

---

[7] Bort, Julie. "The 50 Best Places to Work in 2016, According to Employees." *Business Insider.* December 09, 2015. https://www.businessinsider.com/50-best-places-to-work-in-2016-2015-12#no-8-google-43.

Now its leaders have shifted their focus to the future. Their spotlight for decisions is moving from mobile first to artificial intelligence first.

When leaders act and speak with words that combine the destination with a spotlight and a priority, they set in motion the ability to maximize profits. Let's look at what Google leadership is doing. They set a destination (organize information); they have a spotlight (artificial intelligence first); and they have a priority for decisions (does it help?).

It will be fun, and perhaps a little scary, as we watch Google maximize its profits and take control of their segment of the artificial intelligence age. The next part of this book examines how to maximize and sustain profits.

PART III

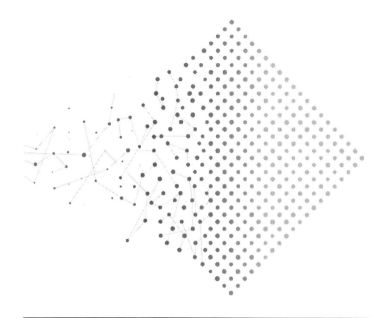

How Focus-Forward Leaders Succeed in Maximizing Profits

CHAPTER 9

4/12/365: The CEO Way Of Doing Business

The idea came in 1990 during a train ride. It was to be a children's book of fiction about life in the early times of England. But the loss of a parent after a long illness, marriage, birth of a daughter, and then a failed marriage left the idea and the book on the shelf. Defeated and penniless, the author moved in with a sibling and began receiving government assistance. The idea took two more years to incubate before it finally became a manuscript.

Five years after the train ride, when the idea was first formed, a manuscript was developed. It was submitted and then rejected by twelve publishing houses. Five years and twelve rejections would be enough to make anyone quit, but in 1995, a small publishing house named Bloomsbury extended a £1500 advance to turn the manuscript into a book. Two years later, in 1997, seven years after the idea was first formed, a meager first run of 500 books was published.

In 1998, J.K. Rowling won the British Book Awards Children's Book of the Year for *Harry Potter and the Philosopher's Stone*, known in America as *Harry Potter and the Sorcerer's Stone*. She won that same award in 1999 with *Harry Potter and the Chamber of Secrets.* In 1997, 1998, and 1999 she also won the Nestlé Smarties Children's Book Prize Gold Medal. Today, she has sold more than 400 million copies of her books. She is now one of the most successful fiction authors in the world.

Without knowing it, the author consistently completed every action item we have discussed. Let's review what happened over that seven-year period. The process began with an idea and the determination to write a children's book everyone could enjoy (desire to accomplish). Dedication to the idea (focus-forward leadership) led to encouragement from other leaders, which led to decisions to remain committed to the next step (rest stops). Every rest stop reinforced the decision (momentum) to continue. The decisions to continue, supported by words of belief, maximized the outcome.

A Straight Line

As mentioned earlier, Ralph Waldo Emerson's words from the 1800s are just as true today as they were then. He said, "All great masters are chiefly distinguished by the power of adding a second, a third, and perhaps a fourth step in a continuous line. Many a man had taken the first step. With every additional step, you enhance immensely the value of your first."

That is what J. K. Rowling did, and that is what focus-forward leaders must do.

Decisions in a straight line, like steps in a straight line, are the most difficult to accomplish. Yet that is exactly what is required, even though realities such as personnel, financing, and market conditions all contribute to less-than-perfect results.

In the chart below, we have depicted what typically happens with companies during a four-year period. When momentum follows the black line, decisions or steps (as described by Emerson) are being made in a straight line. We call it strategic momentum. Results at the end of the year have the greatest potential to show maximized profits.

The solid and dashed grey lines show the impact of reality on a company's ability to make decisions in a straight line. Curved lines are the plan; wavy lines are actual results in this perfect chart world. Both the dashed and solid grey lines demonstrate the impact of reality and the ability of a company to remain focused on what its leaders want to accomplish.

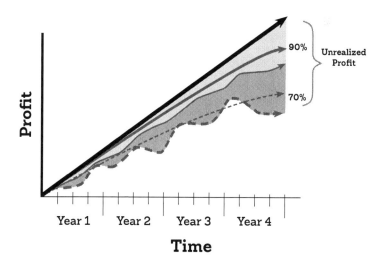

Companies with clear pictures, rest stops, spotlights, and priorities are depicted with the solid grey lines and light grey background. They have better opportunities to maximize long-term profits.

Companies making decisions about many opportunities without the benefit of a clear picture, rest stops, spotlights, or priorities are shown with the dashed grey lines in a dark grey background.

The grey background represents the fact that potential to maximize profits still exists, even though both companies may be enjoying very good or acceptable profits.

As the artificial intelligence tsunami comes closer, companies in the dark grey area will find that competitors with disruptive technologies are also operating in the dark gray area to secure these potential profits for themselves.

Only the creative ability and discipline of focus-forward leaders using the action steps outlined in previous chapters and the 4/12/365 way of doing business can overcome this threat to potential profits. The actions of these leaders will require competitors to adjust to them as a focus-forward company and a market leader.

Why 4/12/365 Is The CEO Way Of Doing Business

The challenge of the coming artificial intelligence tsunami requires an agile way of doing business. New ideas, concepts, and techniques must be quickly assessed within a consistent and effective game plan that will achieve and maintain momentum and maximize profits. Overcoming competitive threats and disruptive technologies starts with what a company's focus-forward leaders do 4/12/365 times a year.

The 4/12/365 process drives decision momentum only one way; that is forward, to maximize profits. The idea is simple: Quarterly. Monthly. Daily. Repeat.

As we depicted with the dashed grey lines in the chart, entrepreneurs will discard the 4/12/365 process so they can be quick and nimble in order to grab every new idea and hopefully grab as much new profit as possible. These business leaders feel that their busyness is momentum. Unfortunately, their results will follow the dashed grey line on the chart above. Their focus is about being *busy*.

The 4/12/365 process focuses on a consistent, yet highly responsive way of doing business on a quarterly, monthly and daily basis. It is not about lessons others have learned, nor is it about best practices that don't work in your company. It is about what focus-forward leaders do in the process of *making things better than it was before they got there*. It requires four summits, twelve meetings, and 365 daily actions that focus on the future. As always, the primary goal is to maximize profits.

Four Quarterly Summits

Everything the focus-forward company does should be focused into four quarterly summits. These summits should be held off-site for the CEO and the top executives. Such summits require trust, openness, and a team dedicated to the outcome they want to accomplish. The focus should be to concentrate only on the way forward.

The first quarterly summit is the annual meeting that begins the company's fiscal year. The work of the off-site should be to confirm the company's core values and its dedication to the five action items, along with questions such as:

- Do leaders know what they want to accomplish long-term? Has it changed?

- How does each of the top executives focus his or her part of the organization to achieve the long-term goal(s)? Do they have the right people to get there?

- Do they know what the rest stops are along the way? Have they changed?

- Are all the top executives committed to reaching the rest stops for this year?

- What priorities will determine decisions?

- How should the leaders focus decisions to create forward momentum?

- What are the unsettled issues that must be resolved to get there? Who needs to resolve them and when?

- How do the leaders focus words and actions to communicate their goals and rest stops to the rest of the employees?

- How do they build consistency that creates employee buy-in to what leaders are doing and where they are going?

These questions and more are the focus of each quarterly off-site. These meetings are even more important at the beginning of a new year. (If you don't know where you are going, how are you going to know if you got there?)

But the answers are not always found in a meeting. Many times they are found in the more relaxed, social time of the off-site. Recall the adage: "All work and no play makes Jack a dull boy." Company leaders need time to relax and get away from it all. They need time to have informal discussions about what the company wants to accomplish as well as to build the understanding that when one succeeds, all succeed in maximizing profits. The off-site is a time to focus on building trust. It goes without saying, the annual off-site sets the tone and the trust for all subsequent meetings throughout the rest of the year.

The remaining quarterly summits are a time of reconfirmation and assessment. There is much to be done. These are times for each leader to reconfirm commitment to achieving the significant action goals committed to at the annual summit—a time for the leadership team to focus their discussions on three items: time, resources, and leadership attention.

Quarterly summits provide a time to improve productivity, communication, cooperation, and awareness. They are a time to assess the efficient and effective use of leadership talent. They are a time of reassessing metrics, reconfirming quarterly priorities, and resolving unsettled issues. They are also a time to reconfirm the spotlight for important decision parameters and a time to assess responsibility and accountability.

The four quarterly off-site summits are essential. Focus-forward leaders must continually revisit their thinking in order to establish a focus-forward company that is dedicated to achieving their goals and maximizing their profits in the artificial intelligence age.

Twelve Monthly Meetings

Monthly meetings are designed to assure that the leadership team and their staffs have not lost sight of what it is that the company wants to accomplish over the quarter and the year. They are a "How goes it?" that looks at quick reference points for how well things are going. Metrics, KPIs, unsettled issues and cross-functional priorities are at the center point of these meetings.

The twelve monthly meetings are where new tools and data requirements are identified and/or evaluated.

This awareness is essential to develop and adjust to artificial intelligence that will maximize profits and move the company beyond the destructive reach of the coming tsunami.

365 Daily Actions

Daily actions are the enthusiasm that discovers new ideas and ways of doing things to maximize profits for the artificial intelligence age. Daily Discipline provides the daily actions to create strong momentum, leading to strong monthly meetings, which establish well executed quarters, positioning the company for another profit-maximizing year.

The CEO Way of Doing Business

To survive the artificial intelligence tsunami, companies must provide more organizational structure around priorities and long-term results. Leaders must link business objectives, performance processes, and people together to drive momentum and increase profits. The five action items and the 4/12/365 process answer this need.

Perhaps a football analogy would be helpful. Football requires both players on the field and coaches to direct the game plan. For many years, coaches had only one view of the game—from the sidelines. They did the best they could, but they kept hearing from fans telling them what they were doing wrong. It turns out the spectator from high in the stands had a different perspective than the coaches on the sidelines. When the coaches saw things from the fans' strategic position, they realized they could adjust the game without changing the game plan.

It is the same in business. Focus-forward leaders are the link between the game plan and the action on the field. From a position above the daily tasks, focus-forward leaders must look at what is going on with their leaders throughout the company, even at levels three or four or five. Focus-forward leaders must adjust to the game without changing the game plan.

Companies that maximize profits in the coming tsunami must use every tool available to develop a predictable company that can react to the challenges of the artificial intelligence age. As we have emphasized with the 4/12/365 process, focus-forward leadership allows leaders to adjust. It requires data, daily discipline, and consistency of application.

Artificial Intelligence Data

Data, along with statistical analysis, is the key to providing the insight necessary for decisions to be made in real time. The game plan will identify the data that is needed. But just as a game plan is limited by the talent of the players, so too is data limited by where it comes from and what it can do.

The initial role of artificial intelligence data is machine learning. Its objective is to look at history and define what is needed for the future. Analysis of monthly internal data should depict where the company is moving to and provide a definition of what is important. Over time, as more data is collected, data analysis should provide a moving picture of where the company has been and where it is moving to.

Using this learning, machines can create push notifications and prediction analytics to help leaders make better decisions. As we described earlier, however, this is just the beginning of the capabilities of AI. Artificial intelligence will become smarter and smarter. Businesses must learn to walk with machine learning before they run. In the artificial intelligence age, the speed and force of the tsunami will require organizations to walk faster and faster and to run soon after that.

CHAPTER 10

It's Up to You

This book contains all you need to know to maximize profits. Spend your time perfecting the five action items and the 4/12/365 process.

Focus-forward leadership is about the future world leaders will work in. This book is designed to build a firm structure and the discipline for an organization to determine the kinds of leaders and data companies will need to compete and maximize profits in the artificial intelligence age.

As a focus-forward leader, I urge you to study this book. Master the five action items and the 4/12/365 process. Gather all its ideas and firmly establish them in your business. Don't listen to conflicting ideas, and don't be pessimistic or adjust the ideas with conflicting resources in the hopes of making it better. Focus-forward leaders will maximize profits because they are using the right ideas and the right data that meets their destination picture at every level of the business.

The artificial intelligence age is upon us. It is big, and it is coming with the force and power of a tsunami that will cause things to change rapidly—perhaps even overnight. Most don't even see it coming, and those who do have badly underestimated its disruptive impact.

Even though the artificial intelligence tsunami will cause much of the disruption, artificial intelligence is not a technology problem to be solved. It is a leadership challenge to lean into. For those with the foresight, there is a way to maximize profits during and after the coming chaos. That way is through focus-forward leadership and the framework in this book.

When leaders fully integrate the five actions and the 4/12/365 game plan into their businesses, they will consistently make good decisions that will overcome the artificial intelligence tsunami. Their decisions will set them up for a future of maximized profits well into the artificial intelligence age.

Focus-forward leaders must build and organize their companies for great accomplishments propelled by those who can grow a business enhanced by artificial intelligence. Leaders with a strong belief in themselves and in what they want to accomplish will define the path for success. Their well-thought-out leadership direction will significantly reduce the amount of tension and unsettled issues that arise during the tsunami and after.

Focus-forward leaders with a destination to work toward, a leadership team willing to take them there, and a set of rest stops along the way enable the mechanism for great decisions by employees at every level of the company. These leaders know that every decision, every priority, and every word must reinforce direction toward rest stops that point to what they want to accomplish.

The rest stops or extraordinary results become beacons to work toward and recognition of achievement along the way to building an enduring legacy. Enduring legacies, reinforced through words of passion and conviction, along with great decisions recognized with words of appreciation and approval, will multiply and expand productivity and the ability to maximize profits.

Enduring legacies reinforce what will be accomplished in the artificial intelligence age. In the end, maximized profits become a byproduct of giving greater value to every customer through the company's capabilities.

The focus-forward leaders who lead as suggested will certainly maximize profits. The profits they receive in return will be in exact proportion to the clarity of what they want to accomplish, their determination to remain focused on their desired outcomes, and the discipline to act consistently.

It is up to you as a focus-forward leader to:

Prepare for the artificial intelligence tsunami

Know it will arrive sooner and be bigger than you think

Be the focus-forward leader who propels your company through the tsunami into the artificial intelligence age

It is with these things in mind that I wish you all the best as a focus-forward leader who is maximizing profits in the artificial intelligence age.

APPENDIX

About The Author

John Robertson is a native Texan who has seen businesses grow and expand for more than forty years. He is a leadership-driven executive who has served in many leadership roles. He is currently the CEO of Leadership ID and Align3, companies he founded in 2008.

John has made a career of developing high-performing organizations. As a corporate president, a retired colonel in the United States Air Force, and a social sector leader, he has developed leaders of significance who continue to develop other leaders to reach their highest potential. His three sons are Eagle Scouts, and their sons are also Eagle Scouts or on the trail to Eagle.

His achievements include building and operating successful real estate and insurance businesses, serving in the Air Force in both active duty and reserve roles, and contributing in numerous leadership roles in his church and other nonprofit organizations.

As the CEO of Leadership ID and Align3, he works with CEOs who want to break out of current patterns and move their company to a higher level. In today's corporate environment, organizations must be flexible, aligned, and ready for the coming requirements of the artificial intelligence age. He is continually working with leaders to meet the challenges of this new era.

John enjoys spending time with his wife and three sons and their families, fly fishing, working with his hands on almost any construction or mechanical project, and traveling as time permits.

WORKS REFERENCED

Bort, Julie. "The 50 Best Places to Work in 2016, According to Employees." *Business Insider*. December 09, 2015. https://www.businessinsider.com/50-best-places-to-work-in-2016-2015-12.

Collins, James C. *Good to Great: Why Some Companies Make the Leap...and Others Don't*. New York, NY: Collins, 2009.

"C-Suite Challenge™ 2018: Re-inventing the Organization for the Digital Age." The Conference Board. April 2018. https://www.conference-board.org/c-suite-challenge2018/.

Dimon, Jamie, and Warren E. Buffett. "Short-Termism Is Harming the Economy." *The Wall Street Journal*. June 07, 2018. Accessed November 09, 2018. https://www.wsj.com/articles/short-termism-is-harming-the-economy-1528336801.

"The Evolution of Artificial Intelligence." www.ubs.com/wm. January 2017. Accessed November 05, 2018. https://www.ubs.com/sg/en/wealth-management/thinking-ahead-in-asia/2017/new-dawn.html.

"The 7 Stages of the Future Evolution of Artificial Intelligence." Talwar, Rohit, Steve Wells, Alexandra Whittington, April Koury, and Helen Calle. *Enterprise Management 360˚*. October 05, 2018. Accessed December 05, 2018. https://www.em360tech.com/tech-news/tech-features/artificial-intelligence/.

Miller, Mark, Lucas Conley, and Yvon Chouinard. *Legacy in the Making: Building a Long-Term Brand to Stand out in a Short-Term World*. New York: McGraw-Hill, 2018.

41193086R00078

Made in the USA
Middletown, DE
08 April 2019